Ignatian Pedagogy for Public Schools

Also Available from Bloomsbury

Ecopedagogy, Greg Misiaszek
Pedagogy, Politics and Philosophy of Peace, edited by Carmel Borg and Michael Grech
Pedagogies of Taking Care, Dennis Atkinson
Wonder and Education, Anders Schinkel
Raymond Williams and Education, Ian Menter
Critical Pedagogy for Healing, edited by Tricia M. Kress, Christopher Emdin, and Robert Lake
Hopeful Pedagogies in Higher Education, edited by Mike Seal
Children, Religion and the Ethics of Influence, John Tillson
Socially Just Pedagogies, edited by Vivienne Bozalek, Rosi Braidotti, Tamara Shefer and Michalinos Zembylas
Critical Human Rights, Citizenship, and Democracy Education, edited by Michalinos Zembylas and André Keet
A Pedagogy of Faith, Irwin Leopando
The Catholic Teacher, James D. Kirylo

Ignatian Pedagogy for Public Schools

Character Formation for Urban Youth in New York City

Benjamin James Brenkert

BLOOMSBURY ACADEMIC
LONDON • NEW YORK • OXFORD • NEW DELHI • SYDNEY

BLOOMSBURY ACADEMIC
Bloomsbury Publishing Plc
50 Bedford Square, London, WC1B 3DP, UK
1385 Broadway, New York, NY 10018, USA
29 Earlsfort Terrace, Dublin 2, Ireland

BLOOMSBURY, BLOOMSBURY ACADEMIC and the Diana logo are trademarks of
Bloomsbury Publishing Plc

First published in Great Britain 2023
paperback edition published 2025

Copyright © Benjamin James Brenkert, 2023

Benjamin James Brenkert has asserted his right under the Copyright, Designs and Patents
Act, 1988, to be identified as Author of this work.

For legal purposes the Acknowledgements on p. ix constitute an extension of this
copyright page.

Cover design: Grace Ridge
Cover image © Klaus Vedfelt / Getty Images

All rights reserved. No part of this publication may be reproduced or transmitted
in any form or by any means, electronic or mechanical, including photocopying, recording,
or any information storage or retrieval system, without prior permission in writing
from the publishers.

Bloomsbury Publishing Plc does not have any control over, or responsibility for, any third-party websites referred to or in this book. All internet addresses given in this book were correct at the time of going to press. The author and publisher regret any inconvenience caused if addresses have changed or sites have ceased to exist, but can accept no responsibility for any such changes.

A catalogue record for this book is available from the British Library.

A catalog record for this book is available from the Library of Congress.

ISBN: HB: 978-1-3503-3901-9
PB: 978-1-3503-3905-7
ePDF: 978-1-3503-3902-6
eBook: 978-1-3503-3903-3

Typeset by Deanta Global Publishing Services, Chennai, India

To find out more about our authors and books visit www.bloomsbury.com and
sign up for our newsletters.

Figure 0 Mural of Maya Angelou that graces the Elijah G. Stroud Elementary School in Crown Heights, Brooklyn, New York

Contents

List of Tables		viii
Acknowledgments		ix
1	The Pedagogy of Ignatius of Loyola	1
2	Ignatius of Loyola and Character Formation	19
3	Feminist Theology and Pedagogy: Engaging Critical Theory	27
4	Assessing a Jesuit-Sponsored School's Afterschool Program of Character Formation	47
5	Special Education Placement (From Most Restrictive Environment to Least Restrictive Environment): An Application of Ignatian Pedagogy and the *IPP* in a New York City Public School	65
6	Ignatian Pedagogy and the *Ignatian Pedagogical Paradigm*: Implications and Findings for New York City Public Schools	79
7	A Framework for Human Flourishing and the Creation of the Beloved Community	87
Notes		113
Bibliography		130
Annotated Bibliography		144
Appendix A: The Jesuit-Sponsored School Afterschool Program of Character Formation Student Survey		155
Appendix B: Hypotheses		162
Appendix C: Results: Student Age and Self-Esteem		163
Appendix D: Results: Student Grade Level and Development of Social Skills		164
Appendix E: Results: Student Age and Intensity of Activity		166
Appendix F: Results: Sense of Belonging		169
Appendix G: Logic Model Situation		170
Index		172

Tables

4.1	Survey Questions	57
4.2	Students' Activity	58
5.1	Special Education Practice (as of May 31, 2019)	68

Acknowledgments

The ones who educate many to justice will shine like stars unto lasting eternities.
—The Book of the Prophet Daniel (12:3)

Become what you are, having learned what that is.
—Pindar

Ite inflammate omnia. **Go forth, and set the world on fire.**
—Ignatius of Loyola

First and foremost, I am extremely grateful to the public school students and staff with whom I have worked throughout my career as a school social worker. Their immense knowledge and plentiful experience have encouraged me to develop this text and to courage me onward to be my best and most true self.

I am especially grateful for the insights of my colleague Gabriella Oldham, who provided essential feedback to me while I completed this book on Ignatian Pedagogy and public schools. I would like to thank Mark Richardson and Anna Elliss, my editors at Bloomsbury Publishing, for their editorial direction and assistance to me, which ensured that this book went to publication and, as a result, reached the most readers worldwide. It is their kind help and support that have made my writing, while working in New York City, a wonderful time.

Finally, I would like to express my gratitude to my parents, Albert James and Loretta Marie Brenkert, my siblings, my friends, the Society of Jesus (the Jesuits), and my husband, Willian A. Brenkert. Without their tremendous love, understanding, and encouragement over the past few years, it would be impossible for me to complete my second text or to become the person who God invites me to be.

1

The Pedagogy of Ignatius of Loyola

1.1 Charting the Course

Please join me on a journey of dialogue and discovery, as Ignatius of Loyola, a sixteenth-century Spaniard (from the Basque region of Spain), Catholic saint, priest, theologian, and the founder of the Society of Jesus (the Jesuits), informs readers about how public schools can deliver their curriculum while operating a program of character formation with their students in the twenty-first century. This conversation is unique, stemming from the Humanist Tradition through the Industrial Revolution to our postmodern world, a world whose systems of education have been forever changed for the better by the Black Lives Matter Movement, the #MeToo Movement, the Climate Change Movement, globalism, and the Covid-19 pandemic. Administrators and educators in public schools can learn much about their students through critical reflection about Ignatius's philosophy of education and his pedagogical paradigm. From the beginning of our journey, I recognize the tradition of the Roman Catholic Church, its role in colonization and the maintenance of slavery, as well as its role in maintaining some oppression/oppressive practices that counter the common good. I acknowledge that for nearly ten years, I was a Jesuit seminarian in good standing, and I left the Jesuit order and formation to be a priest in protest of the firing of gays and lesbians from paid employment and volunteer positions in the church (because they love people of the same gender and sexual orientation).[1] This book is not about the Roman Catholic Church, its doctrine, dogma, theology, or catechism, nor can this book be labeled as a tool useful for evangelization. Rather, it is about Ignatian Pedagogy for public schools and aims at character formation for urban youth in cities like New York City.

The roots of my interdisciplinary studies research lie in my own formative experience of public education in the Valley Stream Central School District, located on Long Island, New York. There, I learned how to be a citizen, part of a multiethnic community whose demographics changed from a majority White population to a balanced mix of White, Hispanic, Asian, and Black Indigenous People of Color (BIPOC) just as I graduated high school in 1998. Nine years later, after a two-year period of novice training and prayerful discernment, I entered the Jesuits. Once a professed member of the Jesuits, I studied programs of character formation in schools. I also witnessed firsthand during my own experience as a faculty member at Saint Peter's Preparatory School (Jersey City, New Jersey) the amazing program of character formation run by North American Jesuit-Sponsored Schools in the Jesuit Schools Network (JSN), formerly known as the Jesuit Secondary Education Association (JSEA)—what Fr. Pedro Arrupe, SJ, the Superior General of the Society of Jesus, called "*a certain Ignacianidad*," essentially the logical consequence of students in receipt of a Jesuit education from one of the Jesuit-Sponsored Schools found throughout the globe.[2] Still, Ignatius of Loyola, the founder of the Jesuits, saw beyond the physical boundaries of his schools; his Ignatian vision has never been limited to the Jesuits. Consider his *Rules for Thinking with the Church* (contained in his *Spiritual Exercises*), where he focused more on and developed a specific plan within the government of his religious order to protect children and to educate students in schools. Over time, he and his religious order grew to be more effective in protecting children and educating students than any other founder or Catholic religious order in the history of the church.

Today, I am employed as a tenured monolingual school social worker for the New York City Department of Education (NYC DOE),[3] working first in Queens and now in Brooklyn. I see great hope for educators using Ignatian Pedagogy in public schools as well as applying the best practices learned from the Jesuit school program (model) of Ignatian Character Formation to public schools, especially those where I have worked for the NYC DOE. I cannot emphasize enough: the NYC DOE has already embraced some ideas of character formation and social-emotional learning programming to the benefit of its students, families, staff, and community, but those programs are not universal. As such, this book does not set out to destabilize the work of my peers and colleagues. As I have completed the required NYC DOE trainings in implicit bias, my project is intentionally complimentary and supportive of the NYC DOE's efforts to character form and character educate urban youth for a future we cannot predict.

There are also different pedagogical (methods of teaching) approaches to learning; for example, in the West are constructivism, social constructivism, behaviorism, liberationism, and critical pedagogic theories that work through curriculum (the content taught) to facilitate and capitalize student learning. In the East are communal methods of learning; for example, the Muslim tradition emphasizes holistic and lifelong learning, while the Jewish tradition emphasizes knowledge of Hebrew and the history of Israel to foster and cultivate a Jewish identity through teaching and learning. Indigenous populations also have their own specific local pedagogies and curricula. There are different curriculum programs, some global like the International Baccalaureate Program[4] that is an inquiry-based and concept-driven transdisciplinary model of teaching and learning. Through this book, I hope to offer insights to readers about a less well-known, though equally global and interdisciplinary pedagogy—Ignatian Pedagogy and its concomitant *Ignatian Pedagogical Paradigm (IPP)*. Ignatian Pedagogy is student-centered and context-driven; it is adaptable within complex urban learning environments and contexts that include character formation programming for public school general education and special education students—all in an effort to see our youth thrive.

For nearly ten years, I have worked in private Catholic schools and public schools as a campus minister, teacher, guidance counselor, and school social worker. There is no question that public and private education helps students to grow as thinkers and to be formed as citizens. Much has been gained by recent advances in the fields of the science of reading, balanced literacy, equity frameworks, and antiracist pedagogy. In contrast to the NYC DOE public schools where I have worked, all Jesuit schools are especially tasked with forming their students to become women and men for others—others being the operative term that describes the least and most marginalized in society. A distinctive trait of Jesuit education is a concern for a foundational acquisition of culture (including through instruction in humane letters) and a spiritual zeal among youth. The Jesuit priest Juan de Bonifacio was recorded by another Jesuit priest and author of a text on teaching, Fr. Joseph de Jouvancy, as instructing teachers to consider "the education of youth to be the renewal of the world."[5] For the student, this renewal is processed interdependently, not prescribed, through the *Ignatian Pedagogical Paradigm*: the educational context leads to experience, experience leads to reflection, reflection leads to action, which takes the form of evaluation. As a result, the student's service to one's neighbors and community members is transformational. A similar experience occurs for the woman or man completing Ignatius of Loyola's thirty-day retreat, which is encapsulated in his *Spiritual Exercises*.

The Jesuit model of schools started in Messina in Sicily in 1548; the public school system in New York became a permanent system in 1812. For over 472 years, the Jesuits have educated youth around the world, with a program that is increasingly praised and respected, wherein girls and boys will learn among their academics these characteristics of education, for example, tools of character formation: *Magis* (defined herein as striving for More); becoming women and men for others; care of the person; unity of heart, mind, and soul; *Ad maiorem Dei gloriam* (for/to the greater glory of God); and forming and educating students to become agents of change. Such a program of character formation continues for those young women and men who decide to attend a Jesuit college or university within the network of Jesuit-sponsored institutions of higher education, known as the Association of Jesuit Colleges and Universities (AJCU), or their sister colleges and universities found around the world.

Why does character formation in public schools matter? For nearly 210 years, the NYC DOE has served and educated youth, attending to the needs of poor, middle-class, working-class, and immigrant families in public schools. In 2020-1, the NYC DOE projected to serve 1,094,138 students in five boroughs at 1,859 schools, including 271 charter schools, with demographics that looked like this: 13.3 percent were English Language Learners (ELLs), 20.8 percent were students with disabilities (SWDs), and 73.0 percent were economically disadvantaged. Some 138,648 students were enrolled in charter schools in New York City. The four-year graduation rate for NYC DOE students was 81.2 percent in 2021. In many ways, each public school is autonomous of the NYC DOE's central government, led currently by Schools Chancellor David C. Banks. The schools where I have worked in Queens and Brooklyn have no universal programs or systems of character formation as instituted by the staff at the Jesuit-Sponsored Schools. I do not suggest that Jesuit-Sponsored Schools have all the answers or are better than public schools; however, they do offer a program of character formation (through practice/praxis) and virtue development (morality) that is worth considering as an application to or in concert with current NYC DOE programming in pedagogy.[6] Nevertheless, I discuss how and why universal programs of character formation can have greater positive effects on the education of public school youth, while also demonstrating the types of support needed to maintain quality and program reach. The absence of such programming in the NYC DOE is a problem worth evaluating, one that is addressed (interdisciplinarily) through this book.

Such an incongruence or a dissonance in programming in the public schools where I have worked has led me to formulate my research question: Could the pedagogical philosophy of the Jesuit founder, Ignatius of Loyola, be used to apply and create a similar program/system of character formation in the NYC DOE schools where I have worked?[7] It is, then, my hope that this research can be used to study the larger implementation and concomitant implications of universalizing a program of character formation in the NYC DOE (and other schools in the universe of large city public school systems). Such a program could parallel, if not partner with, current implicit bias trainings, contentment programming and social-emotional intelligence programming, and culturally relevant pedagogies already implemented and utilized by administration and staff in the NYC DOE. I am aware that universality tends to follow the perspective of the dominant group, not of the marginalized; just as there is no objectivity without a standpoint, there is no universality without a standpoint. Hence, I attempted with indebtedness and gratitude to the ressourcement movement of Catholic renewal,[8] to create a framework for creating the Beloved Community in Chapter 7. Then Covid-19 occurred. As a result, my narrative took on a much more theoretical formulation, with attending pilot studies—all in an effort to provide indicators and recommendations about the possible formative and transformative value of creating an NYC DOE public schools program of character formation based on the pedagogical philosophy of Ignatius of Loyola, as captured by the *Ratio Studiorum* (RS), Ignatian Pedagogy, and the *Ignatian Pedagogical Paradigm*.

To accomplish this work, I set out to present in my chapters the following material. Chapter 1 describes the pedagogy of Ignatius of Loyola, and Chapter 2 examines his ideas about character formation within the context of the literature on this same subject. Chapter 3 addresses concerns about the meeting of faith and education in public schools through the lens (hermeneutic) of feminist theology and pedagogy. This chapter also tackles critical theory by advancing it to an emancipatory, albeit practical, application. Chapter 4 presents a pilot study for one way I helped to evaluate the afterschool programming that would develop and form the students' at a Jesuit-Sponsored School. Chapter 5 specifically examines a pilot study completed at an NYC DOE School, which tracked the placement of five special education students from a Most Restrictive Environment (MRE) to a Least Restrictive Environment (LRE) as a way to build self-esteem and form character—in other words, to help them flourish as individuals and as members of the school-wide community.[9]

Chapter 6 discusses findings and implications for the NYC DOE if they were to consider developing a universal program of character formation based on the programs in place at Jesuit-Sponsored Schools. Special attention is placed on the formative and transformative value of programs/systems of character formation as well as the limitations of such programming in public schools. The conclusion of this chapter recalls what has been accomplished herein and ends on character formation and human flourishing with the prescient words of the poet William Wordsworth in "A Character" (written in 1800).[10] Chapter 7 presents a framework for creating the Beloved Community, my statement for and about how human beings flourish, for example, ascending toward a rationalization for why public and private schools need and will benefit from programs of character formation in the twenty-first century. Though not a lawyer, Chapter 7 sees a philo-theological way to balance the United States Constitution's First Amendment's two clauses on religious freedom, the Free Exercise Clause and the Establishment Clause, such is important because the US Supreme Court decided through a 6-3 decision in the case *Joseph A. Kennedy v. Bremerton School District* (2022) that the government cannot suppress an individual from engaging in personal religious observance, even when that person is on school grounds, for in doing so would violate the Free Speech and Free Exercise Clause of the First Amendment.

Much time and energy have been spent on writing about achievement gaps, student inspiration, differentiated instruction, and motivating NYC DOE youth to learn. Much less time and energy have been spent on developing curriculum that promotes character formation in public schools. Like Ron Berger,[11] I am intrigued by these deeper questions: How do I really know what I have done for students? What have the students done for me? How do I know what my public schools have done for students in the long run? How does one measure, evaluate, and assess something like this? One thing is for sure: in a post-Covid-19 pandemic world, schools cannot be self-protective any longer; they must help: (1) produce students who feel agency over their own learning; (2) empower families toward greater interconnectivity; and (3) forge long-lasting connections between collaborators: (a) community, school, and family; and (b) family, students, and school representatives. Schools, whether Jesuit or public, should have one common purpose through the educational process: the formation of a balanced person with ongoing habits of reflection. Such a healthier, graduated citizenry has vast implications for reducing violence in our world.

Character formation is explained as the way in which youth are formed as whole persons to be in relationship with self and others (and perhaps a higher power of their choosing). They become active participants in a world which emphasizes their flourishing as part of humanity and enhances their ability to be critical, reflective, and self-directed through their psycho-social-environmental well-being. I believe NYC DOE public schools can accomplish this purpose by learning about character formation and human flourishing from the successful model of Jesuit education at Jesuit-Sponsored Schools around the world. In so doing, our NYC DOE public school students can become men and women for others. The analytical educational philosopher Richard Stanley Peters understood character formation, an aim of education throughout time, as important because an individual's character

> represents [his/her/their] own distinctive style of rule following. But it represents an emphasis, and individualized pattern, which is drawn from a public pool (sic culture). Character traits are internalized social rules such as honesty, punctuality, truthfulness, selflessness. A person's character represents [his/her/their] own achievement, [his/her/their] own manner of imposing regulations on his inclinations. But the rules which [he/she/they] imposes are those into which [he/she/they has/have] been initiated since the dawn of [his/her/their] life as a social being.[12]

The production of such citizens would augment the common good and the search for the good life, something US president Joseph R. Biden, who is also familiar with Jesuit education and Ignatian Spirituality, noted in his January 20, 2021, inaugural address when he paraphrased Augustine of Hippo: "Many centuries ago, St. Augustine, a saint in my church, wrote that a people was a multitude defined by the common objects of their love."[13]

1.2 The Pedagogy of Ignatius of Loyola

Ignatius of Loyola's (b. 1491–d. 1556) experience of God led to greater freedom—hence, how he organized his First Principle and Foundation in his *Spiritual Exercises* to reflect his lived reality of freedom. By 1565, the Society of Jesus (the Jesuits) numbered more than 3,500 members, while today there are more than 14,000 Jesuits worldwide. The Society has existed for more than 450 years. In 2013, the first Jesuit Pope, Pope Francis I, was elected to lead the world's 1.2 billion Roman Catholics. Pope Francis, like Ignatius of Loyola, has made Jesuit education and Ignatian Pedagogy, especially in social justice and education, global.

The Society of Jesus officially came into existence with the papal bull *Regimini Militantis Ecclesiae* on September 27, 1540. The *Formula of the Institute* of the Society of Jesus stated that the Jesuits were founded chiefly for this purpose:

> to strive especially for the defense and propagation of the faith and for the progress of souls in Christian life and doctrine, by means of public preaching,

lectures, and any other ministration whatsoever of the word of God, and further by means of the Spiritual Exercises, the education of children and unlettered persons in Christianity, and the spiritual consolation of Christ's faithful through the hearing of confessions and administering the other sacraments.[14]

Over time, the Jesuits' education of children would take place in different settings, such as the gymnasium (teaching language and literature), the college (including the arts), and the university (emphasizing the Jesuit Constitutions). Indeed, the Jesuits instructed lay students in a systematic way, unique to the Society of Jesus. The story of the Jesuits is uniquely tied to the Catholic Counter Reformation and the Humanist and Scholastic Traditions, especially influenced by the great scholar Erasmus of Rotterdam (b. 1466–d. 1536). Ignatius's philosophy of education advocated a purification and transformation of the universal, human, and religious nature of man's relationship with God, the other, and society. Ignatius believed teachers "should make it their special aim, both in their lectures and when occasion is offered outside them, too, to inspire the student to the love of God our Lord, and to a love of the virtues by which they will please him."[15] In 1548, the Jesuits, who were already deeply influenced by the Humanist Tradition and the Renaissance, opened their first school in Messina, Sicily. Many other schools followed; the Jesuit curriculum included Aristotle, Descartes, Moliere, and Voltaire.[16] It was a deeply liberal classical education "in an effort to affect the identity and state of flourishing of the learner."[17] The celebrated founding document and plan of Jesuit education for the Society of Jesus, including its principles and methodology, is titled the *Ratio Studiorum*, published in 1599 and revised in 1616. At its core, the Jesuit educational system was (and now is) inwardly directed (*ad intra*), ultimately for outward (*ad extra*) purposes.[18]

At the inception of the *Ratio Studiorum*, Fr. Claudio Acquaviva was the Superior General of the Society of Jesus. Following the suppression (not excommunication) of the Society of Jesus in 1773 and full restoration of the order in 1814 by Pope Pius VII with the Papal bull *Sollicitudo Omnium Ecclesiam*, the *Ratio Studiorum* was reissued in 1832. The motivation for the mission of Jesuit priests and brothers was to educate the young and to form teachers; their educational philosophy was based on the concept of *Christianitas*, the practice (art) of Christian living.[19] Later, Fr. Pedro Ribadneira, an early Jesuit priest, informed King Philip II of Spain about the purpose of Jesuit schools: "the proper education of youth will mean improvement for the whole world."[20] By the eighteenth century, there were already 800 Jesuit educational institutions, including more than twenty universities. Today, the

Jesuits in the United States organize these institutions into two organizations: the Association of Jesuit Colleges and Universities (AJCU) and the Jesuit Schools Network (JSN), formerly known as the Jesuit Secondary Education Association (JSEA). In the United States, there are twenty-seven Jesuit Colleges and Universities; in both the United States and Canada, there are eighty-eight sponsored Jesuit High Schools, Jesuit Nativity Schools, and Jesuit Cristo Rey Schools. Jesuit education emphasizes individual care and concern for each person, empowers the student to act beyond self-interest (to develop a preferential option [concern] for the poor), and promotes lifelong reflection and openness to growth.

The *Ratio Studiorum* gives life to the *Ignatian Pedagogical Paradigm*, which is now well established as a guidebook (like the TCRWP Units of Study in some NYC DOE public and charter schools) at every Jesuit-sponsored high school, university, college, and grammar and elementary school. The foundational documents of the system and network of Jesuit education, the *Ratio Studiorum* and the *IPP*, do not seek to indoctrinate or exploit students, but rather to promote social justice and the humanization of the poor; they are derived from a religious order where culture and education are friends, not enemies.[21] According to the *IPP*, the teacher and the student have a dual responsibility in the learning process—namely, to think about both teaching and learning.[22] As such, the *IPP* initiates the teacher-learner relationship and predates modern theories about student co-teaching in the classroom with their teachers. The paradigm of the *IPP* is context, experience, reflection, action, and evaluation. The three main principles of the *IPP* are experience, reflection, and action. These principles lead to the person's growth—intellectually, emotionally, and spiritually. The *IPP* is a foundational work for contextual education, while the *Ratio Studiorum* differentiates instruction for students by establishing guidelines for pedagogical approaches (e.g., math and science) and even for the classroom teacher meeting the students' parents. That the *Ratio Studiorum* and *IPP* emphasize contextual education and community interaction is important for addressing many current concerns about how private and for-profit schools impact neighborhoods where, for example, most New York City Public School students return to live, play, and interact with family and friends. Schools are not silos!

To become a teacher is one vocational goal; to be an ethically good person is another. Both depend on a variety of factors that are part and parcel of one's life—some genetic, others social, psychological, or religious. In his seminal text on the philosophy of education, John Dewey wrote:

> An undesirable society, in other words, is one, which internally and externally sets up barriers to free intercourse and communication of experience. A society which makes provision for participation in its good of all its members on equal terms and which secures flexible readjustment of its institutions through interaction of the different forms of associated life is in so far democratic. Such a society must have a type of education, which gives individuals a personal interest in social relationships and control, and the habits of mind, which secure social changes without introducing disorder.[23]

Of course, Dewey's references to order and disorder are narrow, perhaps even unrealistic. Yet, in terms of the desired outcome of successful character formation, to know the Other is an important part of the *IPP* and Dewey's philosophy of education, or rather an important connection/tension—the relationship between the *IPP* and American educational philosophy more generally. Given our political climate today and efforts to impact a free and public education negatively for all students, through vouchers and school choice as examples, there is a need for a democratization of education, for example, equitable opportunity structure through policy changes. By providing New York City Public School students with a program of character formation grounded in the tradition of the *Ratio Studiorum,* many more children will see/experience equitable opportunity and equitable concern for all. Such terms can be likened to Ignatian Spirituality terms: *cura apostolica* and *cura personalis* (respectively, care for the work and care for the whole person, *totus homo*). Of course, stakeholder buy-in is crucial to the success of such programming.

My personal philosophy of education is rooted firmly in Ignatius's educational practice, a process through which faculty, staff, and administrators "endeavor to transmit the ideals of their culture to the young."[24] It is through this process, perhaps better imagined by or as the *IPP*, that young people are led toward their affective as well as efficacious place in the social, national, and religious life of their world, one at once confronted and challenged by a plethora of noises, such as competition for attention from social media, extremism, myths, and groupthink mentalities.[25] Thus, human flourishing is the fruit of the process of education that brings to life the rigors of a discipline intent on shaping the lives of young men and women toward *Magis*. *Magis* derives from Ignatius's meditation on the Call of Christ, from his *Spiritual Exercises*; it is a personal response beyond the wholehearted call to service for and with the Other—that is, the more universal common good. For some who study Ignatian Pedagogy, *Magis* is explained through the terms *creative fidelity, more efficient, more generous,* or simply *the more* or striving for *the more*.[26] *Magis* sees discreet charity and rational service as a means to foster the education of the whole person for what Dewey would call the freedom and fullness of human companionship.[27]

1.3 Ignatius's Chief Educational Ideals

I embrace the core of Ignatius's chief educational ideals, which emphasize twelve elements engaged by my research question: How can New York City Public Schools adopt/adapt Ignatian Pedagogy to create a program of character formation for K-12 students? Ignatius's chief educational ideals, when adapted by the pedagogue, include:

1. The educator has the ultimate objective of stimulating the student to relate his or her activity to his or her final end: the knowledge and love of God in the joy of the beatific vision.
2. The immediate objective of the teacher and the student is the student's deep penetration of his or her field(s) of study, both sacred and secular, for example, cultural synthesis.
3. The Society of Jesus hopes by means of its educational works to send capable and zealous leaders into the social order (secular world), in numbers large enough to leaven it effectively for the good.
4. The development of a scientifically reasoned Christian outlook on life, a Christian worldview enabling the student to live well and meaningfully for this world and the next.
5. That ethical and humanistic studies show how all creation can be directed to God's greater glory and greater self-fulfillment of human beings here and hereafter.
6. To personally contribute to the life of the local community and to the life of the student in the home and school.
7. The formation of the whole person, intellectually and morally.
8. To demonstrate personal interest, care, compassion, and concern, if not love, for students and their progress.
9. To help foster the transmission of multiculturalism and diversity and engage students in creative research and activity.
10. That educators participate in faculty formation and to grow in their roles as, for example, teachers, baseball coach, and guidance counselor.
11. To continuously adapt and evolve the educators' and administrators' procedures and pedagogical methods to circumstances of time, place,

and persons. (This includes formation of stakeholders, including board members, staff, and parent-teacher associations.)
12. To sustain their Ignatian vision and Jesuit mission of educational excellence in the formation of young men and women of competence, conscience, and compassion.[28]

These twelve elements have tremendous implications for my program of study and preparation for work; for instance, how can the NYC DOE, which operates a $38 billion budget, educates more than 1.1 million students, employs more than 135,000 people, and has thirty-two community education councils in a multicultural and urban context, hire and promote like-minded individuals who support the character formation of students for the classroom and beyond? Can the NYC DOE hire and promote employees for mission?[29]

From 1547 to today, the ideals and goals of the *Ratio Studiorum* are indicative of an Ignatian philosophy of education that emphasizes the blending of human flourishing and the discipline of education. As with the seventeenth-century philosopher John Locke, excluding his sexism and racism,[30] the *IPP* deals directly with the intersection of freedom, virtue, kindness, and wisdom in education. I believe that the formation of the entire person, with respect to his or her ultimate goal (human flourishing and relationship with God), and simultaneously with respect to the process of education (the discipline), leads to the person's contribution to society, both as an individual and a member of the universal group called humanity.

To anyone questioning the place of the *IPP* in public education, I offer the text *Jesuit and Feminist Education*, edited by Jocelyn Boryczka and Elizabeth Petrino,[31] as a means of considering how Roman Catholic Schools have integrated the secular and scientific into their curricula. At heart, questions about the separation of church and state are legitimate, especially in an era where the US Supreme Court is whittling that relationship down, for example, to allow for more and more expressions of faith, as personal choice/expression of free speech in many facets of our American lives. Still, Ignatian education has much value to import into public schools, especially in the context of a twenty-first-century, post-industrial, postcolonial, post-Covid-19 pandemic America. The *IPP* becomes an instrument of consciousness raising, something students in public schools can increasingly appreciate, thanks to feminists like Catharine MacKinnon and Judith Butler.[32] As a former teacher and current school social worker, I have always believed in the importance of human beings to flourish freely as individuals and as members of groups, and more specifically as members of the universal group called humanity. As Rousseau believed, I too believe that at its core, education ought to *make good human beings*, a pursuit the philosopher Immanuel Kant understood as seeking moral perfection.[33] Given Kant's racism, it is more helpful and prudent to my conceptualization to spend time with the works of Martin Luther King, Jr., who conceived the making of good human beings through the creation of the Beloved Community. My conceptualization of human flourishing is consistently congruent with reflections about my personal life and the lives of men and women who surround me in my job as a tenured school social worker for the NYC DOE. Human flourishing helps to direct us to the purpose of our life, each in our individual and unique way, as well as to consider how our purpose/flourishing overlaps with other human beings.

1.4 A Problem Question: Can Ignatian Pedagogy and the *IPP* Work in Urban Schools?

Today, there is a crisis in American urban public education. Most of our major cities are populated by racially/ethnically/linguistically marginalized or disenfranchised students whose experience of a free and public education sets them apart from their peers who attend private schools, for example, through inadequate schools, systemic/structural violence (cf. the works of Paul Farmer), tracking, and de facto segregation.[34] Furthermore, public education is losing students to, for example, the branding of private education and an increasingly competitive and selective market for the education of students in charter schools. If the majority of NYC public school children are of color (current demographics indicate the following ethnic breakdown: 40.8 percent Hispanic, 24.7 percent African American, 16.5 percent Asian, and 14.8 percent White), then what cultural considerations are given to them for human flourishing? Still, we can never forget that education is a social process that includes experience, reflection, and action, as contextualized by the *IPP*. Teaching children, which is becoming more data- and evidence-driven, is a one-of-a-kind experience that forever transforms lives and communities. The Jesuit priest Fr. Dean Brackley highlighted seven standards of Jesuit education in which the student should always: (a) strive to understand the world; (b) focus on big questions; (c) be free from bias; (d) help others and oneself discover a sense of purpose (*vocation*), but especially to love and to serve; (e) be diverse and close to the poor—that is, be close to those who experience economic diversity; (f) be true to oneself, deepen one's understanding of truth and faith; and (g) speak, communicate with the wider world.[35]

David Tyack and Larry Cuban ended their seminal text *Tinkering Toward Utopia* by commenting that "Good teachers reinvent the world every day for the children in their classes."[36] There can be no mistaking the utter importance of the roles a teacher and students play in their reciprocal formation. No form of technology, including artificial intelligence, can replicate, replace, or do justice to this relationship. Considering the benefits of introducing a program of character formation for NYC public school students based on Ignatius of Loyola's *Ratio Studiorum* and the *IPP*, we can once again "reassess goals and results in the light of experience."[37] The *IPP* allows for the space for education in the twenty-first century to be active, authentic, participatory, and empowering.[38] The *IPP* allows for teachers to use new, innovative technology and media to shape their students' experience of education, to diversify learning, and to prepare students for the future, all the while employing new technology and new media to create and foster intimate human relationships (cf. how the Jesuit priest Fr. Gregory Boyle uses the *IPP*, Ignatian Spirituality, and new media to work with gangs in the Boyle Heights community in California).[39]

Whether it was Horace Mann who called schooling the "great equalizer"[40] or John Dewey who theorized schools as levers of social progress,[41] schooling has promised an equitable opportunity structure. Ignatius of Loyola looked beyond opportunity to the formation of the whole person for service and work in the world. Today, when we consider our globalizing and interreligious world, we see the benefits of mutual recognition, respect, and interreligious interconnectivity. We understand a common core/connection to human development and human flourishing. The common core/connection to human development and human flourishing falls under/within the rubric of Agape Love that embraces the praxis of the *IPP*.

With all my heart, soul, and mind, I want our children in NYC public schools to flourish by showing them how to love themselves and how to love others. Still, I ask these questions: What about institutional and systemic impediments? Are we placing too much burden on self-recovery on individual shoulders? In Chapter 3, I address the question: How does systemic/institutional change factor into my conception of human flourishing?

1.5 Spiritual Concepts That Influence the Educational Philosophy of Ignatius of Loyola[42]

The following spiritual concepts demonstrate how faith influenced Ignatius's educational philosophy. More importantly, the definition of these concepts enhances the readers' conversation with Ignatius of Loyola as they engage the subject of character formation in public schools.

1.5.1 The Human Being's Relationship with God

For Ignatius, this is a vertical and horizontal relationship: God's gift of Himself to human beings (in time), creating human beings to be in relationship with the Father, the Son and the Holy Spirit in love. The apostolic relationship, discerning love and charity, drawing people into engagement with life and the Kingdom of God, is guided and attuned to the Spirit by a habit of constant, prayerful, discerning reflection.

Finding God in All Things

Ignatius extends the range of images in which God is to be found in the created world. Understanding of created reality: The whole world is seen as an image, which mediates the presence of God to us in various forms. God is really present and active in the world at every level of being.

For Ignatius, the world is a sacrament of God (history/events/objects/beauty of universe communal and personal identity/experience/word/actions/suffering/poverty and hardships).

The whole person is engaged in a process of discernment.

There is an opposition of forces: good and evil (the enemy of human nature).

The Three Powers of the Soul are Memory, Understanding, and Will.

Contemplatives in Everyday Life

The human being is actively finding God in every moment; this equals the accessibility of God. The human being surrenders to God (gratitude and love) by offering (gifts and talents). The human being's growing familiarity with God and awareness of the presence and work of God in the world feed the desire to collaborate with God in this saving work according to the capacity and the circumstances of the person.

Community's ineffable oneness, the human being is charged with serving apostolically in a community of love, in total love and service.

Mystical Foundation

For Ignatius, there is something like an anonymous, unthematic, perhaps repressed, basic experience of God, which is constitutive of man in his concrete make-up (of nature and grace), which can be repressed but not destroyed, which is mystical or has its climax in what the older teachers called infused contemplation.⁴³

For example:

Human beings can experience a holy, loving mystery who communicates its very Self.

God and human beings exist in relationship, God is in love with us, and we are all in love with God and each other.

The human being is a sacrament, Jesus (human and divine), linked to/with God's self-communication of Godself to humanity.

Regarding unity, like Ignatius, our spiritual journeys include mystical purification, illumination, and transformation; loving knowledge; the courageous, total acceptance of life and oneself.

Humanism

Humanism is an approach to life based on humanity and reason—humanists recognize that moral values are properly founded on human nature and experience alone. Ignatius and his companions bonded with the Humanist Tradition through their apostolic spirituality. For Ignatius, the experience of our creation is revealed through sacred text, sacrament, and the teaching of the Church.

Other Points of Interest

Ignatius relates learning to a life virtue and public service, simplification and integration. Faith in the formative and reformative powers of good literature, as well as the mores of individuals and entire societies. Juan Polanco, the Jesuit Secretary for Education, wrote in 1547 that the humanistic approach to studies helped

in the understanding of Scripture, is a traditional [instruction of] philosophy, provides a pedagogically sound entrance into other subjects, enables a person to express his thoughts better, fosters the skills in communication that Jesuit ministries require, and develops the facility in different languages that the international character of the Society demand.⁴⁴

1.6 Conclusion

This chapter introduced readers to Ignatius of Loyola and his educational system, developed further by his Jesuit Order in the *Ratio Studiorum*. It also pointed to the *Ignatian Pedagogical Paradigm* as a pedagogical approach synchronous with public school education. The reader learned about key concepts influencing Ignatian Pedagogy and Ignatian Spirituality.

Character formation was defined as the way in which youth are formed as whole persons to be in relationship with self and others (and perhaps a higher power of their choosing), as active participants in a world, where their flourishing as part of the group called humanity is emphasized and their ability to be critical, reflective, and self-directed is enhanced by their psycho-social-environmental well-being.

The chartered course of a conversation with Ignatius and public school education flows onward to posit a deeper relationship and greater connection between Ignatius's pedagogical philosophy and character formation.

2

Ignatius of Loyola and Character Formation

Human beings are, to a certain degree, the creators of their own meanings of life. Human beings are, to use the theologian Charles Taylor's slogan, "self-interpreting animals: there is no such thing as what they are, independently of how they understand themselves."[1] A human being's understanding of the meaning of their life informs their relationship with themselves and with others, their pursuit of happiness, and their choices and actions. Genuine fulfillment and self-actualization can only be found in something with significance beyond and independent of one's immediate desires (though this is not to say that one's desires and transcendent moral laws never overlap). Human beings have the power to evaluate the worth of their desires. They can aspire to be a certain kind of person; they can aspire to sustain a certain quality of life and to espouse certain noncontingent values. But how are students in, for example, the NYC DOE public schools formed with the tools of character needed to create meaning, to get out of their present experience[2] as needed to pursue human flourishing?

Furthermore, what if students could be agents of the development and formation of their character? For example, what if there was no limit to where they were formed as human beings to participate/flourish in society or to address what is good about their life? This question alone suggests that human beings are not simply brains or minds, while its answers demonstrate that all individuals are unique. Throughout the course of their formal education, students will be exposed to the concepts and strengths of wisdom, knowledge, courage, humanity, justice, temperance, and transcendence.[3] They are exposed to these concepts in schools during the school day, on weekends while spending time within and without their family system, and in the various other places that students can spend time such as the mosque, the church, the synagogue, karate lessons, swimming lessons, baseball, or the Girl Scouts of America. But most students are not exposed to personalized care and concern (*cura personalis*) where, as Metts said, "the teacher becomes as conversant as possible in the life context and experience of the learner."[4]

Students have much to learn in formal education settings and in life, but so do their family members; an objective of instruction and discipline is to "prepare the young for future responsibilities and for success in life," according to Dewey.[5] It has been said that human beings can never stop learning, but that character formation takes place through stages, with some being more successful than others.[6] In 1921, the Jesuit priest Fr. Ernest R. Hull defined character as a "life dominated by principles; and therefore it comprehends all life so far as it can be dominated by principles."[7] Character formation can be defined as an umbrella term loosely used to describe the teaching of children in a manner that will help them develop variously as moral, civic, good, mannered, behaved, non-bullying, healthy, critical, successful, traditional, compliant, or socially acceptable beings.[8] Transforming schools through a curriculum based on "real-life" character formation, and not through some "Grit Scale,"[9] for example, by developing a program where learning is collaborative, creates a more positive learning environment, and fosters the connection between the school, the family, and the wider community.[10] Thus, the motivation is the creation of human relationship, not the emotional and motivational aspects of morality (as conceived by Lawrence Kohlberg in his *Chapters on Moral Development*[11]). Such a program of character formation, as I conceive it, is based in brain research, for example, the science of the mind,[12] and cognitive theory, for example, theories of multiple intelligences as developed by Howard Gardner and David Lazear.[13] Moreover, in my experience of urban, poor youth, holding top-level goals for a long time is problematized by systemic violence and breakdowns in the structures of the delivery of education. For these students, goal conflict is not "a necessary feature of human existence,"[14] but something the American author and activist James Baldwin might describe as necessary to fulfill the needs of White America in his texts, *I Am Not Your Negro* and *The Fire Next Time*.

I reviewed literature on this topic and, consequently, I proposed some initial ideas about the role of character formation in public schools. Programs that foster character formation, and not just strive toward genius-making, aptitude, or achievement, promote student agency, for example, personal ownership over their own learning experiences, improved family empowerment, and forging a long-lasting connection between various collaborators (family, students, school representatives, especially teachers and students). The program of character formation from the Society of Jesus, implemented through the *Ignatian Pedagogical Paradigm* (*IPP*) in Jesuit-Sponsored Schools across the world, delivers on a wide range of indicators of student success. It seeks primarily to create a universal mobility between the student and his/her environment. Through praxis (volunteerism), the students at Saint Peter's Preparatory School, Jersey City, New Jersey, where I worked first in 2007 and again from 2010 to 2013, learned to distinguish virtue, character strengths, and situational themes.[15] Such wisdom cannot be achieved without social intelligence that is gained by the students' (a) observation of surrounding social conditions, (b) an increase of his/her knowledge, and (c) judgment/discernment between wants and desires.[16]

In my work as a doctoral student at Teachers College, Columbia University, I was principally concerned with developing a program of character formation for students who attend NYC DOE public schools. Thus, my vision for creating and implementing my program of character formation is based on evidence, research, and readings in Ignatian education and public education, as well as my own experience as a Jesuit seminarian, my values, and my imagination now as a layperson working as a tenured school social worker in the NYC DOE.

Public schools develop and implement their own mission and vision statements and goals for accomplishing them, all the while responding to chancellors, school boards, and others who request evidence-based data on student performance, all in an effort to stress accountability. By forming their students, public school teachers can erase deficits between learning acquisition and preparing scholars to be members of the community. Thus, schools and families need to humanize the education experience by creating an educational experience centered on character formation. As González, Moll, and Amanti discussed in their seminal work *Funds of Knowledge: Theorizing Practice in Household*, bringing the home into the traditional learning environment improves children's academic and socioemotional skills.[17] However, most schools lack the capacity to forge a meaningful connection with families. As a result of my review of the literature on this topic, programs of character formation serve as mediating forces between schools and families.[18] Programs of character formation can have these goals in mind: (1) fostering student agency in their own learning, (2) empowering families, and (3) developing long-lasting connections between collaborators, namely (a) community, school, and family; and (b) family, students, and school representatives.

Building character is difficult when students do not have their basic needs met. Consequently, one might ask: How might socioeconomic disadvantage factor into this program, especially for racially and socioeconomically marginalized students? Why is it important to bring parents/guardians into this conversation? Some parents are too overwhelmed with the demands of survival to deal appropriately with disciplining their children and helping to build their character in a positive manner. How would a parent program assist in also helping schools form children? The rationale for conceptualizing programs of character formation based on the pedagogy of Ignatius of Loyola includes the need to teach for citizenship, educate participants through real-world experiences, and form human relationships between peoples in systems, for example, enhance family engagement of the school system, while not disrupting the student's relationship with his or her faith or no faith in order to put "school and place of worship" in their cordoned-off space.

In a post-Covid-19 pandemic world, I see the need to create a *new* type of character formation program in the learning environment, where adults and children can learn together in contextual and practical forms. First, as they learn and interact with each other, students and teachers will develop social cognition, social reciprocity, social-emotional intelligence, and the social skills necessary to become good democratic citizens.

Second, with community and family members also participating in the process of education on the local level, for example, through hands-on experiences, student learning will not be limited to the school building or to typical methods of instruction or be bound by multiple measures of assessment. Through participating in programs of character formation, I believe students in public schools can acquire the standards, values, and knowledge about their society. To that end, much of the program design includes a multicultural and contextual pedagogy and curriculum that facilitates learning and the completion of activities of daily living. For example, students will learn skills to cook, budget money, create a garden, and take care of infants and the elderly. Students will be further challenged toward formation of their character by being exposed to the most vulnerable and least among us in society: feeding the homeless, fixing homes affected by severe weather, and working with children and adults with intellectual disabilities.

As a result of these exercises, students can develop their socioemotional well-being; they will be able to bring what they learn from the environment back to their classrooms, communities, homes, and, later, workplaces. In this case, the learning is self-directed and self-actualized, whereas participants acquire the standards, values, and knowledge of their society.

Lastly, the program of character formation that I envision seeks to form human relationships. Like Ignatius of Loyola, a celebrated inventor of a pedagogical paradigm, I seek not only to move beyond *simply* learning to form the whole person but also to create people who know each other on a deep and personal level. Such thinking can be likened to Loyola's pedagogical terms: *cura apostolica* and *cura personalis*. Today, when I consider our globalizing and intercultural world, the benefits of mutual recognition, respect, and interconnectivity are clear. In the face of extremism, we must re-learn to understand that a common core/connection to human development and human flourishing unites us as members of the group called humanity. The common core/connection to human development and human flourishing falls under/within the rubric of Agape Love, which embraces the praxis of the creation of the Beloved Community (see Chapter 7).

Such a program of character formation is needed because it takes as its central aim the promotion of human flourishing (or happiness). Human flourishing can be defined as the realization of one's human potential—more specifically, the realization of one's basic human endowments—in a manner that suits the individual's uniqueness.[19] Human flourishing is important toward meeting this end: living the ideal life as a human being who is also part of a universal entity called humanity. Thus exists the relationship between human flourishing and human nature; as Freire noted, "the pursuit of full humanity, however, cannot be carried out in isolation or individualism, but only in fellowship and solidarity; therefore, it cannot unfold in the antagonistic relations between the oppressor(s) and oppressed."[20] This concept of human flourishing is useful for answering pedagogical questions about what we ought to do about the kinds of human beings we should try to become through schooling.

An accountability system is defined as a set of commitments, policies, and practices that are designed to create responsible and responsive education[21] or a variety of formal and informal ways by which people in schools give an account of their actions to someone in a position of formal authority, inside or outside the school.[22] School leaders and educators are increasingly recognizing that schooling requires a partnership between families-school representatives-students-community members.

Character formation is explained as the way in which youth are formed as whole persons to be in relationship with self and others (and perhaps a higher power of their choosing), as active participants in a world, where their flourishing as part of the group called humanity is emphasized and their ability to be critical, reflective, and self-directed is enhanced by their psycho-social-environmental well-being. Programs of character formation require accountability and program evaluation. A program of character formation based on Ignatian Pedagogy sees itself as being accountable to the common good for promoting human relationships and long-lasting connections between all the members of the school community. There is an internal accountability involving the different collaborators, which would enhance the school's ways of responding to external pressures in productive and coordinated ways. The atmosphere surrounding the internal accountability system would be characterized by the belief that family and community members as well as school staff will have a positive impact on the students' formation of character. The implementation of the program of character formation, albeit as viewed through the praxis and hermeneutic of Ignatian Pedagogy, aims to heighten the probability that improved human relationships and interconnectivity will occur for families, students, and community members and provide the framework for *cura personalis*.

Character formation programming influenced by Ignatian Pedagogy focuses on fostering human relationships through contextual and multicultural education; this is why many families elect to send their children to Jesuit-Sponsored Schools. Thus, the goal is to use the traditional public school building to go beyond pedagogy, assessment, and evaluation. Therefore, to yield best practices, I propose that schools ask these questions, which are easily linked to the *IPP*:[23]

- How are staff, faculty, and administrators hired to deliver the school's vision, mission, and goals?
- How will co-teaching and learning between teacher and student be structured around praxis, for example, through the vertical and horizontal as well as hidden curriculum?
- How will administrative and pedagogic decisions be made, for example, by consensus and collaboration about academic curriculum/professional development and according to student, family, and community needs and interests?
- How will each grade pursue an age-appropriate/developmentally appropriate engagement of the poor or least among us, for example, will fifth graders volunteer at a pantry one time per month?
- How will strategies be implemented to promote continual student inquiry and improvement in student performance, for example, through the delivery of assemblies that deal with topics like climate change?
- How will fundraising for the delivery of the school's vision, mission, and goals impact the school system?
- How will community-based organization (CBO) staff be trained to deliver a synchronous program of character formation, especially if the school day cannot be expanded due to shortfalls in the public school's budget?

Some of the answers to these and other prescient questions can ensure that the program of character formation is consistent with the school's vision, mission, and goals.

2.1 Conclusion

In this chapter, I examined the relationship between Ignatian Pedagogy and character formation, leading to the development of some questions purposeful for the discernment of programming in public schools, which are always aligned with the school's mission, vision, and goals. A literature review assisted readers in deepening their understanding of character formation and why systems of education look to include this in their curricula. I looked ahead toward the development of a universal program of character formation in public schools.

In the next chapter, feminist theologies (as critical theories) are engaged in a way that assuages worries about the role of faith or evangelization in public school education. A program of character formation in public schools, based on the pedagogical philosophy of Ignatius of Loyola, does not have to be catechetical in scope and sequence. Ignatian Spirituality allows for a person-centered experience of an Other, or God, or Higher Power beyond oneself. I propose that students of faith and no faith at all attend public schools and institutions of higher learning; they will also enter the workforce or vocational schools. The idea here is to take the best practices from the success of Jesuit-sponsored high/middle/grammar schools, colleges, and universities and apply them to public schools.

In the following chapter, feminist theologians propose new and challenging understandings of God as feminine, or conceive God as mother, suggesting that thinking outside the theological norm is important to achieve the end of challenging the status quo. As such, readers are invited to continue the journey with Ignatius of Loyola and to imagine how his pedagogical philosophy and concomitant framework for character formation could be successfully implemented in public schools such as those of the NYC DOE.

3

Feminist Theology and Pedagogy

Engaging Critical Theory

From my first literature review, I now set out to go more deeply into character formation by examining its relationship to feminist theology and pedagogy. This is important because it furthers this interdisciplinary approach to answering my research question. In so doing, my framework moves closer to a practical application in public schools, as a method of character formation based on the *Ignatian Pedagogical Paradigm* (*IPP*), explored later in Chapter 4 in the Encore Character Formation Program at a Jesuit-Sponsored School, as well as in Chapter 5 at an NYC DOE public school where students with learning disabilities were moved from the Most Restrictive Environment (MRE) to the Least Restrictive Environment (LRE). In this chapter, faith is here defined as an affective-spiritual dimension of human interaction, which may or may not include a higher power or being. Pedagogy is here defined as an approach to teaching that arises out of the students' experience of reality, with emphasis placed on the *IPP*. The goal is to move toward an emancipatory feminist theory of human flourishing based on the relationship between feminist theology and pedagogy.

In the United States, the Roman Catholic Church first established schools in Louisiana and Maryland during the colonial era. Schools were also founded in the Spanish Missions in California "to dominate, civilize and educate" indigenous people.[1] Later, schools like St. Frances Academy founded in 1828, opened to educate African American youth in Maryland; it is one of the oldest Roman Catholic Schools in the country. By the 1870s, America sought to distance schooling from its parochial nature; schools were further secularized toward the end of a free public school education.[2] The states of Montana, North Dakota, South Dakota, and Washington were admitted to the union only after they "guaranteed their public schools would be free from sectarian control."[3] The goal was to eliminate Catholic influence from public schools. In 1884,

Roman Catholic Bishops "ordered every parish to build a school."[4] Throughout the Industrial Revolution, the country emerged as anti-Catholic, and more laws were passed that limited attendance of students in Catholic schools.[5] By 1964, over five million students attended Catholic elementary and secondary schools,[6] perhaps a Catholic school's Renaissance.[7] With fewer nuns and priests, lay people emerged as the new leaders of the classroom, and the same can be said about the hiring of lay men and women as principals of the schools. Over time, partnership schools grew more and more common as Catholic schools closed because of increased tuition rates as well as the sex abuse scandal and the need for the Church to sell school property to raise funds in response to filing for bankruptcy.[8] As previously discussed, the Jesuits founded many schools and continue to sponsor schools in America today.

If the Covid-19 pandemic has taught us anything, it is that women are the principal in-home and school-based educators of America's children. Such is a conscientization that Paulo Freire could admire. As a former Jesuit and feminist, I know from my personal experience and my academic studies that women remain underpaid and underrepresented in the workforce (e.g., in Fortune 500 companies) and are pushed to the margins by our patriarchal and male-dominated society. I know all too well that women live in a male-dominated world that sees men and women voice strong opinions about women's roles in society, at home, at school, at church, and in many other areas. In 2022, a male and Roman Catholic-dominant US Supreme Court reversed its own fifty-year standing decision and precedent in *Roe v. Wade* (1973) and returned women's reproductive rights to the states in *Dobbs v. Jackson Women's Health* (2022), with justices declaring in a 6-3 decision that *Roe* was "egregiously decided" and that other decisions should be reviewed—decisions about gay marriage, contraception, and possibly interracial marriage. Much is at stake here, specifically the relationship between faith and pedagogy in the public school system. Feminist theology thusly advocates for speaking to power. In the case of this topic of character formation in public schools, it affords an opportunity to question mechanisms of power that would deny God-speak in public schools, whereas a true contextual nature of the classroom would allow students to refer back to their experience of God or to a higher power throughout their education, which should strive always to be intersectional, contextual, and equitable. Thus, again, this chapter builds on the last and seeks emancipation from long-standing historical norms, patriarchal hermeneutics, and male-centered critical theory, particularly within and against movements in the larger discourse of feminism.

The US Constitution does not explicitly seal the separation of church and state in its amendments; rather, it is a legacy of interpretation (as a legal principle) that has codified it through the writings of men like Roger Williams (1644) and Thomas Jefferson (1802), and the US Supreme Court (e.g., *Everson v. Board of Education* [1947]). Most recently, in 2020, the US Supreme Court ruled in favor of three mothers from Montana, who sought to use taxpayer funding to send their children to private, religious schools (cf. *Espinosa v. Montana Board of Revenue*). Whether it is school prayer or school vouchers, faith (not evangelization or proselytization) and pedagogy (method of teaching) do not necessarily go hand in hand, but perhaps they no longer need to be viewed as hostile antagonists. I pose this question: Could the inclusion of faith (not catechism) and pedagogy increase enrollment in public schools?

It is the lack of access to free and appropriate public education, and the stereotype that faith and pedagogy impinge upon a student's First Amendment rights, that nourished my engagement of theological texts during an independent study with Professor Christopher Emdin at Teachers College, Columbia University. It was through a feminist lens that I read, analyzed, and interpreted the works of men like Jonathan Edwards, William James, Horace Bushnell, James Cone, and James Kugel. Like education, faiths implement pedagogies to teach catechism, to character-form believers, and to enhance the flourishing of their religious communities. In my study, I did not seek to overlook feminine contributions to theology and pedagogy, for in that canon of literature, education like faith itself could be seen as a liberator from oppression. Over time, my concern grew to include questions about what feminist theologians were saying about their experience of the divine, about God, about freedom from oppression, even about how they conceived humanity's relationship to God as being crucial to the placement of American theology in its postcolonial, globalizing, and now post-Covid-19 pandemic context. Such voices were important to this chapter, where I looked to establish a symbiotic relationship between faith and pedagogy in public schools.

Perhaps for too long the public education process has ruled out faith and religion from its ongoing educational activity. Certainly, something is missing from public education and public schools that is causing parents to enroll their children in other school settings and learning environments (e.g., charter schools, Yeshivas, and Jesuit-Sponsored Schools). To attempt this analysis, I looked to feminist theology for help. There, I found the works of Radclyffe Hall, Mary Daly, Elisabeth Johnson, and Jeannine Hill Fletcher. The contributions of Hall, Daly, Johnson, and Hill Fletcher are key to my argument that educators cannot deny that for some of their students, faith shapes their lives and transforms their reality. As feminist theologians, these women inspire dialogue about the relationship between faith and pedagogy in public schools. That dialogue is essential to promoting character formation and human flourishing. These feminist theologians challenged stagnant images of God, women, and the other. Their ability to open doors allowed me to have a conversation with my readers about creating a program of character formation based on the *Ignatian Pedagogical Paradigm* in the NYC DOE.

As I surveyed feminist theological texts, I questioned why public school education can be antagonistic toward faith, especially when many of the students and their families value faith, and faith serves as a type of pedagogy for them. If women theologians (albeit Western and Christian) challenged their male contemporaries to be more inclusive, to be more sensitive to women's experience(s) of the divine, of God, of Jesus, even of the Church and religion in American society, then perhaps public school education could become more supportive of the experience of faith and pedagogy in the everyday life of its students. Yet, the disproportionate representation of women in the history of theological thought is endemic of our male-dominated world, one steeped in a Western tradition of thought beholden to Greek philosophers, Roman polity, St. Thomas Aquinas and the Middle Ages, members of the all-male Roman Catholic Magisterium, and other heteronormative and White male-dominant intellectual patriarchs.

Hence, my interest here is to analyze synthetically four very different yet very important feminist texts. They were chosen not only because of their originality but also because of how I conceive of them as bridging feminist theology and pedagogy. I propose that my program of character formation is enhanced by the voices of feminist theologians and the feminist hermeneutic, who/which represent the motherly intuitions of our students' primary caregivers and in-home educators. The relationship between women and pedagogy cannot be overstated. Thus, my framework now gravitates toward an emancipatory feminist theory of human flourishing, whose application through programs of character formation is further explored in subsequent chapters.

Each text selected encompasses a different literary form, such as Victorian literature, philosophical theology, hermeneutics, and comparative theology, and four distinct voices from Radclyffe Hall's proto-feminism onward to Jeannine Hill Fletcher's feminist conversation about interreligious dialogue. Before I discuss the four seminal texts by Radclyffe Hall, Mary Daly, Elizabeth Johnson, and Jeannine Hill Fletcher, I place feminism in its American (historiographic) context.⁹ By the end of this chapter, I argue why faith and public education should no longer be asynchronous and that it is possible to create and implement a program of character formation based on Ignatian Pedagogy in a public school system like the NYC DOE. To do this, I begin with a brief survey of the history of feminism in the United States.

In the United States, feminism, feminist theory, and its corresponding social justice movements, actresses, and activists have moved through three distinct and important waves. In the United States, the first wave occurred from the late nineteenth century and ended in the mid-twentieth century; the second wave lasted from the 1960s to the 1990s; and the third wave spans the mid-1990s to the present. I consider each wave of feminism as having a seminal historical moment: the first wave and the Seneca Falls Convention; the second wave and the sexual liberation of women vis-à-vis the Civil Rights Movement and the Gay and Lesbian Liberation Movement; and the third wave and postmodernism, where the emphasis is on the deconstruction of male-dominated binaries and hermeneutics and the reconstruction of gender-neutral typologies.

At all times and during all three waves, feminism and feminist theorists attempted to reconcile women's inequality, subordination, male privilege, and women's domination by men. The global course of feminism has looked at moral boundaries, for example, the powerful and powerless, and proposed an Ethic of Care. Today, television shows and movies—from the popular HBO series *Sex and the City* (1998) to the Netflix series *Orange Is the New Black* (2013); movies *Vicky Cristina Barcelona* (2008) and *I Care A Lot* (2021); and the Showtime original series *The L Word* (2004) and *Masters of Sex* (2013)—reveal postmodern society's desire, if not a broader appeal, to understand feminine desire, emotion, and human sociability. Who could ever forget Victor Hugo's heroine, Fantine, from his *Les Miserables* (1862)! What about feminism's contribution to the acquisition of knowledge, or pedagogy, as opposed to discipline of children? Certainly, schooling is not merely understood as creating good habits, as children were once taught to recite the Lord's Prayer.¹⁰

At times radical, at other times accommodating to men, feminism has attempted to eradicate masculine hierarchies and kyriarchies;¹¹ it has sounded democratic and Marxist, assimilating and subversive, poetic, phenomenal and metaphysical, and so on. Over time, feminist authors and theologians have attempted to reconcile monistic and masculine images of God, seeking to find a voice and a vocabulary that speak about Eastern and Western women's experiences of God—all in an effort to improve women's human flourishing. After all, both men and women are made in the image and likeness of God (Genesis 1:26-7).

In so doing, these men and women have attempted to reevaluate universal values and happiness. Moreover, in pursuing an emancipatory feminist theory of human flourishing, one can locate a universal definition of human flourishing that everyone can support.

Throughout this chapter, the following definition orients readers: an emancipatory feminist theory of human flourishing is defined as the liberated and empowered realization of one's human potential—more specifically, the realization of one's basic human endowments—in a manner that suits the individual's uniqueness as well. Generally, human flourishing is important toward meeting this end: living the ideal life as a human being who is also part of a universal group called humanity. It is a desire for the eternal peace and happiness of life.

Despite having met success and failure in their argumentation, how do Hall, Daly, Johnson, and Hill Fletcher speak about human flourishing? This question is especially poignant when one considers their different approaches. Hall uses lesbian fiction to write about women in same-sex relationships; Daly treats metaethics (antagonistically) through radical feminism; Johnson does not address the metaphor of mother and motherhood in her hermeneutical examination of pluralistic metaphors for naming God; and Hill Fletcher provides a comparative theology useful to establishing criteria for interreligious dialogue. The answers to this question demonstrate both the nearness and the distance from which these four feminist authors attempt to revision a society that celebrates women and feminine human flourishing. With Mary Daly in mind, let us begin with what she termed an "intergalactic journey," and see how these feminists opened up dialogue, thus allowing for a possible conversation about using the *IPP* in public schools to develop and create programs of character formation based on the pedagogy of Ignatius of Loyola.

Can two adult women love each other? Can they express their relationship by holding hands in public or having consensual sex in private? How do parents rear or treat a daughter who might be a lesbian? How can I reconcile my sense of who I am with a God who loves me as I am? These are the questions at the heart of Radclyffe Hall's 1920s classic of lesbian, religious fiction. Originally published in 1928, *The Well of Loneliness* captured the public by storm. Hall's novel quickly and controversially went through an obscenity trial, which ultimately censored it for "not having stigmatized 'this' relationship as being in any way blameworthy."[12] Yet, the impact of Hall's lesbian novel was far less harmful than those written by her contemporary gay novelists.[13] For some, Hall's novel represents one particular aspect of sexual life, as it exists among us today;

for others, the book represents a timeless classic; and still, for others, both are represented in this novel.

From the 1950s on, critics pondered whether Hall's novel furthered the work of sexologist Havelock Ellis or whether Hall simply colored the landscape of fiction with her protagonist Stephen Gordon. Primitive studies of *The Well of Loneliness* provided pages upon pages of lesbian analysis. The sexual revolution allowed critics and academics to consider the erotic nature of Hall's work; however, much of the debate saw Hall merging gender and sexuality into inversion—that nameless, unnamed, and pathologized state-of-being. Nevertheless, Hall was freer to write about same-sex sexual desire because she was not beholden to the Magisterium like Elizabeth Johnson. Hall could write freely about lesbianism and erotic love, God's love for these women, while Mary Daly introduced an intergalactic journey that was so radical and at times so very hard to follow that the meta-narrative was lost in translation. Yet, the conception of human flourishing and human good in the classic lesbian text *The Well of Loneliness* helped Radclyffe Hall explore the relationship between human nature, human individuality, and group membership. Hall, writing in Victorian England, told us quickly through her protagonist Stephen Gordon what I believe to be true about human flourishing—that human flourishing is and has always been objective, individualized, or diverse, self-directed, and social.[14]

For Hall, the aim in her novel, through a deeply enmeshed narrative voice, was to find some common ground about the universal experience of sexual identity and same-sex sexual desire, so that entrance into dialogue about one's sexual identity can lead to the improvement of human flourishing and not the marginalization (or ostracism) of individuals or groups. With Hall's *The Well of Loneliness*, sexual disability[15] was subjugated by its Victorian and male-dominated culture. Today, feminists re-narrate, re-organize, and re-interpret this subjugation and victimization through the hermeneutical lens of kyriarchy, colonization, and empire. In this case, Victorian England could only accept a hidden or veiled gay or lesbian, whereas public displays of affection were attributed to homosociality.

Hall respectively examined the challenges of evil to human flourishing; later, we will see Hill Fletcher use motherhood as metaphor to frame interreligious dialogue and interreligious interconnectivity. Let us continue with this question in mind: Was Hall acting accommodatingly when she questioned whether her protagonist Stephen Gordon could choose who she was? Or was Hall blind to the fact that Victorian England was not ready to accept same-sex sexual desire?

Note, for instance, the trial of Oscar Wilde—of which Hall was certainly aware (cf. *Regina vs. Wilde, 1895*).

Thus, very early in the twentieth century, Hall troubled the traditional and Victorian definition of family. The traditional and Victorian definition of family was defined as consisting of a husband (male), a wife (female), and their children; today, this is no longer the predominant picture of family life in the west. Today, less than 30 percent of all families are considered traditional, and traditional families are often referred to as the nuclear family. Even Mary Daly in her text *Gyn/Ecology* (1978) considered the "mysticalization" of the mystical body/family in purely phallocentric and patriarchal terms;[16] she warned women against false inclusion and false polarization as she evaluated female friendship.[17]

But what if Hall was too clever for her Victorian audience? What if she was writing to expose her audience to the resilience she herself acquired through the struggle to discover and understand her own sexuality and to comprehend her gender? Note Stephen Gordon's questioning of whether she was a man. Look at the implications of Hall's own prose:

> Came the day when Mary refused to see Martin, when she turned upon Stephen, pale and accusing: "Can't you understand? Are you utterly blind—have you only got eyes now for Valerie Seymour?" And as though she were suddenly smitten dumb, Stephen's lips remained closed and she answered nothing. Then Mary wept and cried out against her: "I won't let you go—I won't let you, I tell you! It's your fault if I love you the way I do. I can't do without you, you've taught me to need you, and now . . ." In half-shamed, half-defiant words she must stand there and plead for what Stephen withheld, and Stephen must listen to such pleading from Mary. Then before the girl realized it, she had said: "But for you, I could have loved Martin Hallam!" Stephen heard her own voice a long way away: "But for me, you could have loved Martin Hallam." Mary flung despairing arms round her neck: "No, no! Not that, I don't know what I'm saying."[18]

The complicated nature of Stephen and Mary's relationship suggests that Hall did not write against how she viewed the naturalness of lesbian desire. The delicacy of their intimacy, the struggle for their identity, supported Hall's defense of lesbians belonging to society, a society that cared for and accepted them as participants in human society. Hall suggested what education should be: the interaction of the learner with his or her environment, learning how to learn, the classroom facilitating human relationships, just as espoused by the *IPP*—to aspire to self-sacrifice to become women and men for others.

Hall's character Stephen Gordon exemplifies self-sacrifice par excellence. What if one reads *The Well of Loneliness* as a meditation on the existential nature of the coming-out process? The coming-out process leads to self-determination and individuation; the creation of a new identity affirms one's ontological connectedness. But Hall missed an opportunity to speak directly about this; therefore, I address the ideas with knowledge and self-discovery in my discussion on Mary Daly. Please keep this question in mind: Regarding the historical problems between a male-dominated society and women's roles in it, did Daly need to formulate a radically different metaethics, constituted by radically different norms and authoritative on radically different grounds?

Why do men continue to dominate women? Why are male sources for research on history or masculine prescriptions for social norms so coercive? What about women? Can women not do it alone, without men? To answer these questions, I situate Mary Daly within the context of the actions of the Radicalesbians who saw no place for regressive feminism. In doing so, I demonstrate how Daly radically illuminated a philosophical theology that has both practical and theoretical applications, one that confronts institutional and religious hierarchies.[19] Daly was fed up with a softer approach to feminism; she was blunt, and to some men she was cunning, baffling, and powerful—if not dangerous. (Mary Daly took on the establishment at Boston College, where she was a tenured professor.)

As a result of Daly's metaethics, women and lesbians felt less "love deficient" and more authentic. Through their writing, lesbians felt a deep sense that their mirrored selves revealed something larger than the self, something belonging universally to God's creation: to be acting, thinking, and flourishing human beings. The Radicalesbians through their philosophy of belonging do not articulate that: (a) lesbians can become like their heterosexual counterparts, (b) lesbians want to become men, and (c) women and lesbians should desire masculine values. Rather, the Radicalesbians seek belonging through conscious socialization (a hermeneutics of conscientization and transformation in the spirit of Paolo Freire), through a cultural revolution that sees new masculine tropes accept women relating to and with other women. From the Radicalesbians, the second wave of feminism turned evermore to culture and to ethics, to meta-narratives. Through the work of women like Daly, radical feminism reformulated the public domain and discourse about a liberated woman. As such, in the 1950s, understanding of same-sex sexual desire and its concurrent lack of analysis of the effects of male domination on women would now be lost. Now, women would champion the cause for the passage of the Equal Rights Amendment (first proposed by Alice Paul and Crystal Eastman, introduced in the US Congress in 1923).

Yet, in her quest to provide the truth about male domination of women, Daly embarked on a journey that had no room for men; she was blinded by the rules of her metaethics. While Daly saw her intergalactic journey as an eliminator of ignorance just as she set up a criterion for epistemology, her provocations placed hearing as the vehicle through which readers could re-create the herstory of the Sacred Text. Men were aghast. How could men move swiftly with her *beyond God the Father* to something like *God the* Mother—and why did Elizabeth Johnson not later mention this in her text? Daly wrote, "Every woman who has come to consciousness can recall an almost endless series of oppressive, violating, insulting, assaulting acts against herSelf. Every woman is battered by such assaults—is, on a psychic level, a battered woman."[20] Was Daly's metaethics the only possible vehicle for the journey? What about Hill Fletcher's proposal that motherhood be used as a dialectic for interreligious dialogue?

Daly (1978) warned against "mythic [superstitious] Christian procession toward God,"[21] whereas the objects of knowledge include: knowing how to do something; knowing objective facts about things, persons, and places; having intimate personal knowledge of persons and interpersonal relationality; and knowing socially constructed categories. Each form is acquired somewhat differently. For Daly, radical feminism promotes an epistemology that sets meta-patriarchy and metaethics ablaze; she grounded her approach in the ends of friendship. Daly radically confronted her male-dominated society, with her intergalactic quest landing at the Second International Symposium on Belief in Vienna in 1975. Daly delivered a paper titled "Radical Feminism: The Qualitative Leap Beyond Patriarchal Religion" while wearing a tiger t-shirt.[22] Where Hall hid herself in her narrative and prose, Daly was free! Freedom and knowledge acquisition are the cornerstone of Ignatian Spirituality as well as the foundation of my Emancipatory Feminist Framework for Human Flourishing.

Daly defined Gyn/Ecology as a verb or a movement where one's awakening helps them to know objective facts about things, persons, places, nature, among others. For Daly, this knowledge normally takes a propositional form or Rage: I know that a 10-billion-dollar pornography industry inspires chauvinism and sexism; I know that Daly wrote to expose atrocities perpetrated against women and that new reproductive technologies continue to develop, and so on. Daly believed that *Woman-Identified Woman* could only happen through radical feminism because men had colonized women and led them astray, where internalized self-hatred festered.[23] Daly cited Adrienne Rich who wrote,

"In bringing the light of critical thinking to bear on her subject, in the very act of becoming more conscious of her situation in the world, a woman may feel herself coming deeper than ever into touch with her unconscious and with her body."[24] Thus, knowledge about oneself requires truth, belief, justification (warrant), and reliability. While truth, belief, and justification are (normally) necessary and sufficient for knowledge, I believe that reliability—the idea that one's justification rests on a reliable process—adds a cognitive check or review to the mental process by which knowledge of objective facts becomes the knowing of objective facts. Daly understood this, which is why she frustrated patriarchal knowledge by distancing herself from the gendered language of "he." Daly wrote:

> When women become aware of the manipulable ambiguity of the pronoun he, we have perceived only the foreground of grammatical silencing techniques. Just as it would be a mistake to fixate upon the pseudogeneric *man* and assume that terms such as *people* and *person* are "real" generics (a falsehood disclosed by such expressions as "people and their wives") so it is a mistake to fixate upon the third person singular. As Monique Wittig has shown, the pronoun *I* conceals the sexual identity of the speaker/writer. The *I* makes the speaker/writer deceptively feel at home in a male-controlled language.[25]

From Daly's efforts, it is better that an emancipatory theory of human flourishing locate the acquisition of everyday propositional knowledge through these forms of experiential knowledge: perception, introspection, memory, reasoning, and testimony. With perception, I know that a rose smells. With introspection, I can tell when I am tired. With memory, I can remember my cell phone number. With reason, memory, and experience, I can explain how a car starts or why structural violence is wrong. With testimony, I can know the time, and I know that masculine pronouns can grammatically silence women.[26]

From Mary Daly, Monique Wittig, and other heroines of the "Second Wave of Feminism," we know that negative labels and categories, including common pedagogical role-assumptions, can be critiqued for anti-universality in the following ways: (a) by locating testimonial injustice and bias; (b) by checking the reliability of myths, opinions, and stereotypes against reason, as well as empirical/scientific study (e.g., qualitative and quantitative scientific/social analysis); (c) by evaluating openness to dialogue; (d) by assessing the epistemic vice or virtue of the hearer; and (e) by investigating the limiting effects of negative labeling on human flourishing. Finally, it is clear to me that as a free and critically reflective human being, I can accept or reject a negative label or category, just as public schools cannot implement the *IPP* because of its historical relationship to God-speak.

I now approach hermeneutics (interpretation), having grounded Mary Daly's philosophical theology in a process of feminist inquiry and evaluation. The task of this hermeneutics section is to use Elizabeth Johnson's 1992 text *She Who Is* to present her methodology of interpretation, which provides criteria for evaluating and judging the moral appropriateness of pluralistic metaphors for God, social labels, and the behaviors and institutions based on those labels. Though a step in the right direction, I believe Johnson's texts represent an accommodating approach to feminism, albeit liberatory, and the appropriateness of the *IPP* in public schools, because of its responsibility to shape the traditional Roman Catholic dialogue about knowing or naming God. From Johnson, I propose that we can evaluate the fit of the *IPP* for NYC DOE public school programs of character formation.

Unlike Hall and Daly, readers can hear Johnson deploy a feminist language that looks to include men. Johnson's language is accessible to men, and Johnson sees men as partners in dialogue. Johnson rightly pointed out: "The dilemma of the word God itself, however, is a real one and not easily resolved."[27] More broadly, Johnson's presentation is important because it also helps in the response to the suffering, pain, and hurt caused by people who call, insult, or label other people as objects based on arbitrary characteristics (e.g., B!^*h, D!>e, F@&&ot, N#&&er, K!>e, F@$$y). Clearly, Johnson is proceeding to find an entrepot into dialogue with men about naming or labeling God; her approach is very different from Hall's literary style of Hall or Daly's radical language. Johnson wrote:

> Images of God are not peripheral or dispensable to theological speech, nor as we have seen, to ecclesial and social praxis. They are crucially important among the many colored veils through which divine mystery is mediated and by means of which we express relationship in return.[28]

Unlike Hall or Daly, Johnson suggested that society has rules based on labels; labels imply conceptual metaphor, for example, images of God, analogy, and conceptual blending. Some discrimination and labeling are appropriate, such as when we tell a legally labeled criminal sex offender that he or she cannot live near a school. But what happens when we attempt to call God Mother or She or to contemplate Jesus as a woman? Or in the case of this project, what happens when we directly ask: Can the *IPP* be employed in public schools without power structures raising concerns about God-speak (or even catechesis) in the classroom? Johnson wrote:

Since it is women whose bodies bear, nourish and deliver new persons into life and, as society is traditionally structured, are most often charged with the responsibility to nurture and raise them in maturity, language about God as mother carries a unique power to express human relationship to the mystery who generates and cares for everything.[29]

For some, Mother-God confronts the absolute mystery of the Triune God; for others, it is starkly anti-Magisterium and therefore harms the truth about Father-Church, even though the metaphor is always "Mother Church." Now consider the relationship between Stephen Gordon and Mary Llewellyn in Hall's text: What are the political implications of Gordon and Llewellyn's subjectivity? Hall wrote:

Then they stood very still, grown abruptly silent. And each of them felt a little afraid, for the realization of great mutual love can at times be so overwhelming a thing, that even the bravest of hearts may grow fearful. And although they could not have put it into words, could not have been explained it to themselves or to each other, they seemed at that moment to be looking beyond the turbulent flood of earthly passion; to be looking straight into the eyes of a love that was changed—a love made perfect, discarnate.[30]

The incarnation of love elicits sympathy from an audience that knows Stephen's burden burns deeply within her soul. As for Johnson, God causes women to be: "In the strength of her love she gives her name as the faithful promise to be there amidst oppression to resist and bring forth."[31] Johnson then helps me to suggest that if God-speak can be for everyone, the *IPP* could be for every classroom—something I believe Ignatius of Loyola would support. The *IPP* allows for every teacher and every child to know each other as individuals. Over time, religion has been used for counter-intuitive purposes, such as promoting slavery in the United States. Fears about the oppressive nature of institutions, like schools, cannot be dismissed. Yet, the *IPP* reminds us that we cannot disconnect from history or context; the universe is real. Some students come to school with relationships with a God or a higher power, and I believe we can embrace such relationships by exploring programs of character formation in the NYC DOE without letting the *IPP* become a method of proselytizing or catechesis. It is evil that we must caution against, not an all-encompassing, all-inclusive formation of youth for the promotion of human flourishing.

Moving onward, I look at Jeannine Hill Fletcher's 2013 text *Motherhood as Metaphor* toward the end of suggesting Hill Fletcher's way of reducing the effects of evil through forgiveness, toward seeing the natural human desire for companionship as foundational to interreligious dialogue. Second, I look at Hill Fletcher's text toward the end of integrating my own masculinity into a feminist approach to interreligious dialogue and interreligious interconnectivity. These steps are important to locating how Hill Fletcher's works assist in promoting the possibility of character formation programs in the NYC DOE in a multicultural, multireligious, and no-religion learning environment. To proceed: I find integrating philosophy and theology helpful. It is noteworthy to remind readers that Hill Fletcher is advancing the current "Wave of Feminism," for which she is indebted to her foresisters, whose voices either were veiled, radical, assimilating, or accommodating.

First, I create the term *Eve-il* to designate and locate the patriarchal and kyriarchal damnation of women (and narrative ambiguity) in Eve, who in Genesis is blamed for falling prey to the serpent and for lusting after the forbidden fruit.[32] Hill Fletcher wrote:

> One note for unsettling the heteronormativity that haunts Eve is her proclamation "I have produced a man with the help of the Lord" (Genesis 4: 1). The mother of all the living does not credit her heterosexual partner for the children she will bear; she credits the divine power. In order to destabilize Eve from Christian heteronormativity, we need to enlist the help of Eve's advocate and the woman through whom Eve herself is recapitulated: Mary.[33]

But to move on from here, rather than defend God's actions in Eve's life, I show how Hill Fletcher reduced the effects of Eve-il by noting that this process need not lead one to give up faith, but rather to seek out interreligious solidarity. It is Eve who represents symbolically all women, it is Eve who bears the burden of labor pains, who first cares for children. Hill Fletcher wrote:

> From this perspective, women and men are both subject to a power and a knowledge system that is rooted in their relationships, and both are constrained by the power that courses through those relationships. Together they demonstrate the human condition of relationality and creativity under the constraint of a knowledge system imbued with differentials of power.[34]

From here we might ask: How does the *IPP* promote who public school students are to become? Or in the language used at Jesuit-Sponsored Schools, what are the characteristics and qualities of the grad-at-graduation?

Nevertheless, belief (or faith) in God or some higher power provides helpful resources for dealing with suffering and evil that unbelievers lack. As has already been seen, feminist theology calls us to see continuously in the "Other" (who is often a victim) the very image and likeness of God; this is a foundational characteristic of the *IPP* and Jesuit education.[35] When considering interreligious dialogue, Hill Fletcher could have asked: Can men and women do this without acknowledging the banality of Eve-il? How do people who believe in God respond to the presence of Eve-il in the world, especially if Eve-il includes the suffering caused by a male-dominated society, for example, through structural violence and discrimination?

We can see Hill Fletcher's response to these questions where she summarized Johnson's perspective on Eve-il:

> In Elizabeth Johnson's vision, God's recreating presence in the world includes the integrity of nature, the liberation of peoples, the flourishing of every person, and the shalom of the whole world in rescue from the powers of evil, which foster sin and destruction.[36]

For Hill Fletcher, the feminist response to Eve-il includes: (a) working to eliminate Eve-il that deprives men and women the capacity to flourish; (b) responding to the causes of structural violence (and to people who accept inappropriate labels) with mutual recognition and respect; (c) taking Eve-il as an opportunity for individuals and groups to call on God, to be merciful, and to forgive rather than to retaliate; and (d) acknowledging the need for trust in God because Eve-il is a mystery bound up with God's intentions. To respond to Eve-il requires forgiveness.

Forgiveness will be revisited in Chapter 7, where I reinforce it conceptually as part of the framework for creating the Beloved Community in which forgiveness rests in the power of the victim. Forgiveness yields: (a) removal of hostility; (b) charity and compassion; (c) the possibility of and for apology and contrition; (c) reintegration of the Eve-ildoer into the life of the individual or group; and (d) the promise of benevolent relationship, including ones with God and other members of the community, based upon mutual recognition, respect, and human flourishing. Goods of forgiveness for the victim and for the perpetrator include mutual recognition and respect; both increased mutual recognition and respect promise new beginnings at the time of new dialogues about sameness and difference between individuals and groups. Of course, forgiveness is bipolar as well—the perpetrator has to accept the forgiveness and internalize it.

It is without question that Hall, Daly, and Johnson wrote in a world that preceded the War on Terror, globalization, and even the development of trade in cryptocurrencies. Their world had borders and boundaries; this is not true today, for our post-Covid-19 pandemic reality has altered space and time forever.

Still, the global War on Terrorism of the last decades provides a helpful backdrop to my discussion about Hill Fletcher's interreligious dialogue. In the global War on Terrorism, a plurality of religions and religious institutions find themselves in conflict. By labeling all Muslims as "possible threats to national security" and all Christians as "the good guys," society fits members of these two groups into artificial categories/labels and roles: terror suspects and heralds of freedom. Hill Fletcher wrote:

> The structure of these interreligious encounters provides witness to the relationality that is fundamental to our human existence, our human condition. The Maryknoll encounter in China reminds us of a foundational premise for interreligious dialogue: We meet one another in multiplicity. We meet not as "religious others" alone but in the complex embeddedness of our lives. That we meet in multiplicity holds the further illumination that we are in multiplicity. The nature of the human person is that we are complex, structured by the wide variety of relationships that create us.[37]

Given the public school versus charter school debate, programs of character formation in the NYC DOE can be part of the solution, with the *IPP*'s ability to transform students through a curriculum based on the pedagogy of Ignatius of Loyola.

In derogatory ways, the negative labeling of, for example, the place of faith or God-speak in public school classrooms transmits false beliefs about particular members of the group or even, more broadly, about that group in general. Antagonism between religious and nonreligious people evolves from a lack of mutual recognition and respect. Interreligious interconnectivity and interreligious dialogue bring people to a discussion about such issues as belief or nonbelief in a higher power and our common humanity. Our common humanity enables members of different religions to recognize each other by their individual and species capacities and labels and as members of God's creation who share in the Sabbath and the possibilities envisioned by Agape Love.[38] Critical feminist pedagogy, much like the *IPP*, sees the emancipation of students through contextual and multicultural education.

Hill Fletcher's understanding of motherhood as metaphor applies to character formation and feminist pedagogy, which I believe promotes human flourishing in several ways: (a) by acknowledging that all men and women are children of God, thus ends in themselves; (b) by calling on different religions and different religious leaders not to politicize debate or treat members of other groups as mere means; (c) by emphasizing that a community of love and brotherhood cannot come into being without the fully moral behavior of all members; and (d) by recognizing structural violence and discrimination for temporary success at best. Interreligious interconnectivity and interreligious dialogue make it possible for mutual recognition and respect to help men and women set aside self-interest, and to see that unity and solidarity are more important than extremism, factionalism, and tribalism.[39]

Interreligious interconnectivity and interreligious dialogue enable us to see the needs of human beings as the needs of our brothers and sisters, and to identify the dangers of social evil, which prevents human flourishing. The diverse and plural needs of our brothers and sisters can then be defined as internal religious diversity. As Hill Fletcher wrote:

> "Internal religious diversity" can refer, then, to religious diversity within a given tradition as well as to the diversity of practice and belief that constitutes the individual at different times of her life. Our recognizing this reminds us to hold "religion" not as a static reality but as a living and dynamic category woven into complex lives.[40]

Accordingly, Hill Fletcher understood that knowledge of false labels about our complex and messy human lives—for example, about a particular religious person, or a spiritual or religious journey, or about a group—allows critical inter- and intra-group reflection to produce vast social change. Of these ideas about comparative theology, Hill Fletcher is useful for promoting the idea that implementing the *IPP* in NYC DOE public schools is possible. Hill Fletcher wrote:

> Our religions do not capture all of who we are. The approach of "sharing stories" witnesses a richer and more complicated approach to interreligious dialogue, as it reminds us that "religion" cannot be reduced to doctrines and scriptures, to "what I believe" or "what I do". "Religion" is always "found" embedded in and intertwined with other aspects of our lived condition: economics, gender, social relations, material conditions, politics, and so forth. Our "religious" identities are entangled in and impacted by all of these features and more.[41]

With interreligious interconnectivity and interreligious dialogue come the mutual recognition and respect for those marginalized (or ostracized) by structural violence and discrimination.

The opposite of this is indifference, and that is passivity at its worst. I end this chapter by returning to the relationship of faith and pedagogy. Faith, not religion, when tied to my concept of an emancipatory theory of feminist human flourishing, supports my belief about synchronicity in the relationship between faith and pedagogy. This is what I learned by investigating feminist theology and pedagogy.

3.1 Conclusion

Certainly, some groups of public school students cannot flourish because the US Constitution separates faith from religion; as Paulo Freire reminded us in 1984, there is a political nature to education. Public schooling as an institution cannot flourish if students do not enroll; during the Covid-19 pandemic, private schools, including Jesuit-Sponsored Schools, were attracting students away from the "broken public school system." The relationships between faith and education, and praxis and education, are two reasons why mothers might seek to place their children in private schools. The proto-feminist and feminist theologians examined in this chapter provide a helpful context for resolving the problem of my study: Can the public school system in New York City create and implement a universal program of character formation based on the *Ignatian Pedagogical Paradigm*?

I believe that an emancipatory theory of feminist human flourishing helps direct individuals and groups toward the purpose of our lives, each of us in our own individual and unique way, as well as overlapping with other human beings.[42] Faith, not religion, can be that pedagogical lens through which education can be treated as a *liberating enterprise*, not a broken system, which reminds us that every person has worth and value, that education cannot be limited to the transfer of data or facts. It is a misnomer that the best citizens are developed from a neutral education system. How can students learn about Agape Love without intersecting it with faith? Without seeing pedagogy and faith as synchronous forces in the education of students, many minority students will remain disadvantaged—for while faith is about neither religion nor conversion, it is about the way in which a group of people perceives reality and exists in solidarity. Again, this is a type of conscientization that Paolo Freire could agree with: allowing the oppressed to experience reality as it is manifested.

Agape Love, developed further in Chapter 7 as part of my framework, has practical and pragmatic expressions, but as a pedagogical concept-in-action, as the *IPP* might suggest, it needs to be grounded in the intersection of faith and pedagogy. Hall, Daly, Johnson, and Hill Fletcher told us through their own feminist, cultural, and linguistic analyses of marginalization and liberation that the effects of structural violence, discrimination, and shame can be reduced, even eliminated, by embracing goodwill, albeit solidarity with and for all people. Faith and pedagogy are synchronous; our human condition propels us onward.

Education, like theology, cannot be empowering unless students see themselves as agents of change; this is what I hope readers will learn by placing Hall, Daly, Johnson, and Hill Fletcher in conversation about human flourishing, pedagogy, and character formation. Just as these feminist theologians opened up a conversation about women's experience of God, so might their legacy actuate such a discussion (without fear) about implementing the *IPP* and creating a program of character formation in NYC DOE public schools.

The next chapter considers my program evaluation of one Jesuit-Sponsored School's Afterschool Program of Character Formation. Our journey with Ignatius will take us through this pilot study to learn about a successful afterschool program and how Ignatius's pedagogical philosophy engages students of faith and no faith at all in a Jesuit-Sponsored School.

4

Assessing a Jesuit-Sponsored School's Afterschool Program of Character Formation[1]

4.1 Introduction

This chapter demonstrates how the students at a Jesuit-Sponsored School, anonymized herein, are formed through Ignatian Pedagogy, including the *Ignatian Pedagogical Paradigm* (*IPP*). Thus, this provides one example of Jesuit education, inclusive of afterschool and summer programming, and its relationship to character formation and human flourishing. My pilot study qualitatively and quantitatively reviewed the Jesuit-Sponsored School's Afterschool Program of Character Formation, referred to herein as the Afterschool Program of Character Formation. My interest in researching the afterschool program at the Jesuit-Sponsored School grew from a desire to reflect to the school administration and staff just what the students (total student population $n = 57$, all boys, mostly from African American and/or Latino families) were saying (self-reporting) about the Afterschool Program of Character Formation and life in their city generally. A literature review introduces readers to the theory and pedagogy behind afterschool education and programming. For this study, I used an anonymous survey (total questions = 59), where the research design included subscales. The survey looked specifically at a student's self-esteem, self-worth, and academic and behavioral performance. The survey was based on the California Healthy Kids Survey 2005, California Department of Education After School Program Survey ASPS-Exit, Fall 2006, Grades 4–6. I administered the survey as a test on March 12, 2009. The evaluation recommended that the Jesuit-Sponsored School should more formally integrate the Afterschool Program of Character Formation into the administration's school-wide curriculum review. Readers of this chapter will better: (a) understand the relevant bio-psycho-socio-econo-enviro-spiritual forces character forming youth in the Jesuit-sponsored middle school and (b) see the need for afterschool programming for at-risk youth and adolescents as a means to promote their flourishing.

4.2 Objectives and Background Literature

In the autumn of 1977, a Jesuit priest met with a team of educators and affected community members to discuss the problems of low-income students and to discern ways to help them. Some twenty-one years later, in May of 1998, the same team of educators proposed to build a school based on the model of an already existing Nativity School in New York City. The decision to build led to the creation of the Jesuit-Sponsored School; the groundwork for the new school was laid in the 1998–9 academic year. The Jesuits agreed to sponsor the school.

The Jesuit-Sponsored School, founded in 1999, is a middle school for boys in Grades 6 through 8, with a maximum of twenty-two students per grade. The first class of sixth graders started at the Jesuit-Sponsored School in 1999; a seventh grade was added in 2000, and an eighth grade in 2001. The Jesuit-Sponsored School graduated its first eighth grade class in 2002. The school's mission is to serve boys who have the potential for college preparatory work, but who are in danger of failing to achieve that potential because of poverty, residence in distressed neighborhoods, or other social or economic factors.

The Jesuit-Sponsored School is a member of the Nativity Network of schools. There are forty-nine such schools in nineteen states, including the United States and Canada. At the Jesuit-Sponsored School, most students are not Catholic. The Nativity Network experiences a high school graduation rate of 89 percent; 62 percent of graduates are placed in college. The average length of the day is 9.5 hours; the school year is extended. The average daily attendance rate is 97 percent.[2]

At the time of my study, a certified teacher and school administrator coordinated the Afterschool Program of Character Formation. Every Jesuit-Sponsored School student selected two classes per quarter from course options including, but not limited to, Band, Cooking, Robotics, Theater, Chess, Art, Boy Scouts of America, and Basketball. These are not discrete offerings nor are they focused on a single subject matter; this is programming that develops and forms character through a culturally relevant pedagogy and curriculum.

My program evaluation assessed the Afterschool Program of Character Formation's outcomes, as they relate to the Jesuit-Sponsored School's primary goal of student formation. According to the Jesuit-Sponsored School's *Student and Family Handbook*:

> The primary goal which Jesuit-Sponsored School sets for all of it students is admission and success at a college preparatory high school, leading to success

in college and the opportunity to contribute as an adult citizen. . . . The Jesuit-Sponsored School is committed to serving young men who will in turn be committed to serving others: to the greater honor and glory of God.[3]

During my study, the Jesuit-Sponsored School was evaluating and writing the first school-wide curriculum for core courses, for example, math and science. The school-wide curriculum review covered the regular school day but did not extend to a review of the mandatory Afterschool Program of Character Formation.

Characteristics of the Afterschool Program of Character Formation include an afterschool education and enrichment program that incorporates: a Monday/Wednesday and Tuesday/Thursday schedule of course offerings (e.g., robotics, basketball, and arts activities), followed by a daily snack time, study hall, and afternoon assembly, which are in turn followed by the dismissal of students. The program runs from 3:09 p.m. to 5:40 p.m., Monday through Thursday.

In terms of research questions, my evaluation was needed to determine whether the Jesuit-Sponsored School should more formally integrate the Afterschool Program of Character Formation into the current school-wide curriculum review. Does the Afterschool Program of Character Formation merit a more formal evaluation for effectiveness? The Afterschool Program of Character Formation operated distinctly from the regular school day. However, there was no curriculum and no formal objectives or goals for key stakeholders, including parents, students, staff, administrators, and board members, to use in analyzing the effectiveness of the Afterschool Program of Character Formation.

Some of the demographics of the participants included:
*57 students in Grades 6 (16), 7 (21), and 8 (20)
*96.4 percent African American, 1.8 percent Caucasian, and 1.8 percent Asian
*All students are Christian; most are not Roman Catholic
*Students' age:
9.1 percent—eleven years old
27.3 percent—twelve years old
40.0 percent—thirteen years old
23.6 percent—fourteen years old
*Students in the seven-year program, which included alumni receiving high school tuition assistance, came from thirty-five different zip codes.
*41.8 percent of students felt safe in their neighborhoods most of the time.
*50 percent of students did not receive less than the grade "C" in a single class during the second quarter of the first semester.

4.3 Literature Review

4.3.1 Introduction to Afterschool Education

My interest in this program evaluation stemmed from: first, trends in the economic downturn experienced locally by African American children;[4] second, the significance of sixth through eighth grade education in the formation of students' interest and love of education; third, a growing interest in the field of character formation and the *Ignatian Pedagogical Paradigm*; and fourth, an effort to see if the Jesuit-Sponsored School was fulfilling its mission and purpose. I was also interested in looking at what survey responses might say about boys and the diversity of African American boyhood. *New York Times* columnist Charles M. Blow evidenced trends in African American Black children in his article titled "No More Excuses?"[5] (January 23, 2009). In *Afterschool Education: Approaches to an Emerging Field*, Noam, Biancarosa, and Dechausay wrote that successful afterschool curricula are:

1. child-/youth-centered, designed to meet the interests of children and youth;
2. open-ended, with flexible goals;
3. built around goals and objectives that go beyond specific academic skill-building to address social-emotional, health-related, and life skills.[6]

David von Drehle called us to believe in our young boys in his *Time Magazine* article entitled "The Boys Are All Right."[7] Thus, while the Jesuit-Sponsored School afterschool program theoretically promotes the full social, psychological, physical, moral, and spiritual development of its students, the aim of this literature review is to introduce readers to afterschool education and enrichment program theory and pedagogy.

Afterschool education is a growing field of specialization, with financial resources shared among local, city, state, and federal governments. Afterschool programs grew in response to changes in American society, which saw parents, especially single parents, at work for longer hours during the regular school day.[8] Students at risk, like those at the Jesuit-Sponsored School, witness disadvantages at a greater rate than their peers.

At-risk students may be defined as those who are physically or emotionally abused and often fight against routine and order, including the school system;[9] they are often disproportionally referred for special education and related services. Of course, along with philosophers like George Yancy, we might purport that order is a trope of whiteness.[10] Still, afterschool programs provide students with transitional and holding environments.[11] The following features of afterschool programming promote positive development for youth: (a) physical and psychological safety; (b) appropriate structure; (c) supportive relationships; (d) opportunities for belonging; (e) positive social norms; (f) support for efficacy and mattering; (g) opportunity for skill-building; and (h) integration of family, school, and community efforts.[12]

Afterschool programs are designed to help students to complete homework, develop social skills, raise awareness of differences (e.g., cultural), and assist parents in becoming partners in their children's education.[13] Students who find themselves in afterschool programming do better in school when non-parenting adult mentors and peer role-modeling provide a basis for a more productive life.[14] As an intermediary space, the afterschool setting is fluid and distinguishable yet at times hindered by what it is not.[15] Afterschool education and enrichment programs cannot replace the home environment; however, it can provide students with opportunities to grow and to develop emotionally, interpersonally, and intellectually. The literature review includes a look at the Missouri State Afterschool profile and core content areas.

4.3.2 Impacts of Afterschool Education

To promote socialization skills, emotional competence, character formation, and human flourishing, Roger P. Weissberg, Karol L. Kumpfer, and Martin E. P. Seligman integrated prevention science with practice methodology.[16] In looking at the impacts of afterschool programs, Susan Goerlich Zief, Sherri Lauver, and Rebecca A. Maynard[17] looked at the extent to which access to afterschool programming impacts student participation, whether afterschool programs vary by subgroup and a group's baseline characteristics, and which programs are more beneficial to youth.[18] In their study, Zief et al.[19] noted the negative effects of unsupervised time between the hours of 3 p.m. to 6 p.m. Measured outcomes were clustered in five areas: student context, participation in enriching activities, behavioral, social and emotional, and academic outcomes. Zief et al. wrote that their study was the first to use a meta-analytic method through pooling evidence of program impacts across studies. The researchers noted that about six million (11 percent) school-age youth participated in afterschool programming in 2002–3. The study suggested that more traditional afterschool programs (e.g., tutoring) might benefit youth, but the impacts were not significant; moreover, alternative models of afterschool programming must be tested, especially within target populations (e.g., at-risk youth).

Students perform better academically when they belong to a school culture that supports the local community and culture and respects diversity in the youth's homelife.[20] Moreover, students who drop out or leave school do so at the end of a long process of disconnectedness, disengagement, and deportment in school.[21] Social workers, educators, and administrators must be aware that cuts in afterschool programming can have negative consequences.

For example, in 2008, the afterschool community had a proposed $300 million cut to afterschool education, contributing to advocacy among organizers and community organizers to advocate on behalf of afterschool education for youth (from 3 p.m. to 6 p.m.) throughout the United States.[22] The Afterschool Investments Project (2009) was sponsored by the US Department of Health and Human Services Administration for Children and Families Child Care Bureau. Afterschool Investments profiles the state of afterschool for every state and allows each state to compare needs, services, and activities across the country. It is a resource for policymakers, administrators, and providers.[23] These organizers advocated on behalf of youth to prevent the cuts. Ultimately, policymakers and advocates noted the positive influences of afterschool programming and how it supports families, communities, and our nation.[24]

4.3.3 Missouri State Afterschool Profile and Core Content Areas

In Missouri, there were 614,205 children ages five to twelve in 2008 (currently over 750,000 children in 2022) and the total federal and state Child Care and Development Funds (CCDF) totaled $131,293,361 in 2008—an estimated $214.00 per child.[25] From the Missouri State Afterschool Profile, the following accomplishments in support of afterschool education and character formation programming are noted: the introduction of a governance board to administer network activities; the development of the Kansas and Missouri Core Competencies for Youth Development Professionals; the creation of the Missouri Afterschool Program Standards; the introduction of the Missouri Afterschool Program Self-Assessment tool; the creation of the Missouri Afterschool Resource Center; technical assistance to support licensure and accreditation; an afterschool curriculum designed to support Missouri State educational standards; and the formation of the Missouri Afterschool Action Plan.

The eight core content areas included in the Kansas and Missouri State Core Competencies for Youth Development Professionals supported findings in Fashola, Noam et al., and Deutsch.[26] The Kansas and Missouri State Core Content Areas of character formation and the promotion of human flourishing are: (a) child/adolescent growth and development; (b) learning and environment curriculum; (c) child/adolescent observation and assessment; (d) families and communities; (e) health, safety, and nutrition; (f) interactions with children/youth; (g) program planning and development; and (h) professional development and leadership.[27]

Finally, in 2007, then Missouri governor Matt Blunt recommended, by himself, $1 million for afterschool programs (e.g., math, science, and health). The effort to fund afterschool programming was initiated by the Missouri Statewide Afterschool Network. The Missouri State legislature-approved funding led to the creation of two new afterschool initiatives—METS (Math, Engineering, Technology, and Science) and Healthy Lifestyles programming—that addressed poor nutrition and childhood obesity. The legislature funded each initiative at $500,000, for a total of $1 million. Late in 2007, the governor announced that his 2008 budget would include an increase to $1.1 million for the afterschool programs.[28]

4.3.4 Creating and Sustaining an Afterschool Program

Gil Noam et al. suggested that unified programming, or programming that bridges the regular school day and the afterschool program, "seamlessly incorporates the best of both worlds."[29] Noam and Fiore articulated the importance of relationship building between students and staff in the afterschool program in the growth, learning, and healing of students.[30] Again, this is routine practice at the Jesuit-Sponsored Schools. Clearly, families, schools, and communities must work in relationship to address the growing needs of students who find themselves in afterschool settings.[31] Moreover, afterschool programming can greatly enhance a boy's self-esteem and sense of self-worth.[32]

Olatokunbo S. Fashola gave social workers, educators, and administrators the theoretical framework to create and build an effective afterschool program. Fashola, Noam et al., and Deutsch looked at community-based afterschool programs, like the New York City Beacons, Los Angeles' Better Educated Students for Tomorrow, New York's East Side Boys and Girls Clubs, and the Boston School Age Child Care Project.[33] Methodology included qualitative research designs: focus groups, interviews, projects, observations, and quantitative studies. It was clear that boys and girls (and gender nonbinary students) experienced both school and everyday life differently (e.g., gender differences, styles, and types of learning and play).[34] Afterschool programming enhances the ways in which boys and girls enter into relationships with the opposite sex.

4.3.5 Conclusion

Consensus in the literature supports the following points: (a) afterschool hours should be structured differently from the regular school day, although bridging the regular school day and the afterschool program is idealized; (b) fun, mentoring, and enrichment should be a part of the afterschool experience; (c) programs should support academic learning; (d) programming should experiment with alternative forms and styles of learning; (e) programs should encourage connections with self, community, and school; and (f) programs should empower students toward self-determination, self-efficacy, and the setting of personal learning goals and objectives.[35] These efforts to promote the well-being of children were supported by findings in Dauber, Alexander, and Entwisle; Miller; and Noam and Fiore.[36] Zief et al. acknowledged that more systematic research needs to be done to review program impacts.[37] They recommended extended data collection, the implementation of complementary process evaluations, and improved study reporting. Noam et al. indicated that more needs to be done to support children who spend about 80 percent of their time outside of school and need afterschool programming to help them prepare for adulthood.[38]

In the previous chapter, readers learned of the importance of freedom regarding the main goals of the *IPP* and Jesuit education. The liberatory nature of Ignatius's pedagogy cannot be overlooked; as Metts wrote, "growth in the responsible use of freedom is facilitated by personal relationship between student and teacher."[39]

4.4 Methodology and Research Design

My data collection plan was an evidence-based, anonymous, mixed-methods survey, looking to assess the efficiency, outcome/impact, and design and theory behind the implementation of the Jesuit-Sponsored School's Encore Program in Character Formation. Elements of the framework included: description of the program, focus on the evaluation design, gathering credible evidence, justification of conclusions, and information dissemination.[40]

The purpose of my data collection plan was twofold. First, I intended to analyze the effectiveness of the Jesuit-Sponsored School Encore Program in Character Formation in relation to school-wide goals for character formation and the Missouri Province of the Society of Jesus objectives for the Jesuit-Sponsored

School to meet the standards of a Jesuit-Sponsored School. Additionally, I intended to promote and justify the evaluation of the students' views about the afterschool program, in part to detail how the students saw the program helped them to flourish as part of the school-wide community and to allow them to self-advocate and be self-efficacious.

To do this, I administered the survey, which was modeled after the California Healthy Kids Survey 2005, California Department of Education After School Program Survey ASPS-Exit, Fall 2006, Grades 4–6, and an additional Jesuit-Sponsored School Student Survey from 2008, reflecting student understanding and valuation of the afterschool program through eight sections and fifty-nine questions.

The survey design was reliable in that it measured the same criterion (e.g., students' self-esteem) across Grades 6 through 8. It was valid because data received from the survey can be compared by age group, by question, or by grade. The reliability and validity of the research design helped measure the hypothetical predictions contained in the first graded assignment. The research design supported external validity in that inferences made through the findings/discussion may be applied to other area NativityMiguel network middle schools and afterschool programs.

The data collection plan assessed whether there was a logical relationship between the variable (student evaluation) and the proposed measure (survey).[41] Note, too, that the sample was the entire student body, with each student present during the administration of the survey and completing the survey. The survey included subscales (total student population $n = 57$). The survey was culturally sensitive, based on personal work at the practicum and research on afterschool education in minority settings. I administered the surveys to the sixth, seventh, and eighth graders at the Jesuit-Sponsored School on March 12, 2009.

My project was Exempt-Behavioral: (a) no children or adults were harmed by the research design, and (b) no medical interventions or treatments were included in the data collection or as part of the study. My research did not use preexisting data because this was the first evaluation of its kind as performed at the Jesuit-Sponsored School; there was no direct observation of students as part of the evaluation.

My research was conducted in an already established educational setting that included standard educational practices. I focused on the afterschool program and questioned whether the Jesuit-Sponsored School should further evaluate the curriculum of the Afterschool Program of Character Formation in relation to the school's use or lack of use of the *Ignatian Pedagogical Paradigm*. Thus, the research focused on the implementation of curricula.

As the principal investigator, I explained the survey instructions to the students, clarifying the goals and objectives of the survey and noted its anonymity and confidentiality. To minimize additional risk or harm, I asked the faculty to review the data collection plan/survey before I implemented the design. Students did not benefit from remuneration. Only I had physical access to the survey data. Benefits to participants included a better experience of the Afterschool Program of Character Formation, greater options for programming, and merited recommendations for an evaluation of the afterschool curricula and its goals and objectives. Individual participants were treated with dignity; the students' human flourishing (well-being) was ensured via the principles of: (a) respect for persons, (b) beneficence, and (c) justice.[42]

4.5 Findings/Results

To test my hypotheses,[43] I used bivariate statistics to look at how the Afterschool Program of Character Formation affected/influenced the relationships between: (a) student age and self-esteem (chi-square); (b) student grade level and the development of social skills (One-Way ANOVA); (c) student age level and intensity of activities performed during the Afterschool Program of Character Formation (chi-square); and (d) sense of belonging among twelve- and thirteen-year-olds in the Afterschool Program of Character Formation (Independent t-test). The total students surveyed was $n = 54$; two students were absent the day the survey was administered.

4.5.1 Student Age and Self-Esteem (Chi-square)[44]

Question: Does the Afterschool Program of Character Formation promote self-esteem?

Increasing students' self-esteem is an informal goal of the Afterschool Program of Character Formation and the Jesuit-Sponsored School in general. To assess whether students believed the Afterschool Program of Character Formation promoted self-esteem, I asked three questions about goals and abilities, to which students could respond No, Maybe, or Yes. I then looked at the relationship between age and self-esteem (see Table 4.1 for results). The percentage of students who were age eleven was 9.1 percent; age twelve, 27.3 percent; age thirteen, 40 percent; and age fourteen, 23.6 percent. When rounded to the nearest age group, the mean age of students was thirteen (mean = 12.78).

No students ($n = 54$) responded "No" to any of these three questions. The findings suggested that students had a high sense of self-worth. Given that no student responded "No" implied that students believed in themselves and might be unable to articulate deficiencies or desire not to promote a negative self-image.

4.5.2 Student Grade Level and Development of Social Skills (ANOVA)[45]

> Question: Does the Afterschool Program of Character Formation promote the development of social skills?

For this question, I compared the mean between student grade levels and the development of social skills. I wanted to see how the students perceived the Afterschool Program of Character Formation helped them to: (a) get into less trouble at school, (b) avoid fights, (c) get along with others, and (d) do better on their report card. Despite the sample size, there was a significant relationship between sixth, seventh, and eighth graders ($p = .040$) who believed the Afterschool Program of Character Formation helped them get into less trouble in school and make new friends ($p = .002$). A less helpful finding was the significance of how the Afterschool Program of Character Formation helped students make friends between groups ($p = .414$). This was helpful to note since the composition of

Table 4.1 Survey Questions

Age of Student	Number of Students Who Replied Yes/Total Students in Age Group
Yes, I can do most things if I try . . .	
11	4/5
12	12/15
13	19/22
14	12/13
Yes, there are many things that I do well . . .	
11	4/5
12	14/15
13	21/22
14	12/13
Yes, I have goals and plans for the future . . .	
11	3/5
12	14/15
13	21/22
14	11/13

Afterschool Program of Character Formations consisted of students from each grade and age level.

4.5.3 Student Age and Intensity of Activities Performed During the Encore Program of Character Formation (Chi-square)[46]

Question: Do Afterschool Program of Character Formation activities increase intensity as students age in the program?

For this question, I looked at the percentage of students across the age span to determine what activities they self-reported and what they were spending most of their time on during the Afterschool Program of Character Formation (see Table 4.2).

From these statistics, it can be inferred that students self-reported spending more time during Encore on nontraditional and nonacademic activities. These statistics reflected student desire for how they wanted to spend time during

Table 4.2 Students' Activity

Activity	Percentage of Students Spending Most of Their Time
Reading	
11	5
12	7
13	9
14	3
Writing	
11	13
12	7
13	3
14	3
Sports/Games	
11	10
12	33
13	32
14	28
Praying/Talking to God	
11	52
12	4
13	14
14	16

the Afterschool Program of Character Formation. That 52 percent of eleven-year-olds ($n = 14$) responded spending most of their time praying or talking to God raised questions about their responses, perhaps reflecting the Hawthorne effect. In this case, the Hawthorne effect might suggest that the Jesuit-Sponsored School students taking the survey improved on their answers and performance by reacting to the examiner or to the questions—they could have felt threatened or feared that privileges might be taken away.

4.5.4 Sense of Belonging Among Twelve- and Thirteen-Year-Olds in the Afterschool Program of Character Formation (t-test)[47]

Question: Does the Afterschool Program of Character Formation increase the sense of belonging for students' age twelve and thirteen years old?

The means in this t-test reflected how students aged twelve and thirteen responded on average to questions about their sense of belonging to the Afterschool Program of Character Formation and being part of the Jesuit-Sponsored School community. Students responding "Some" to the questions about this sense of belonging and being part of the community indicated that their sense of belonging was not entirely secure. According to the Levene Test for Equality of Variances, (a) the most significant response came in the question "Does the Encore staff believe that you can do a good job?" (Sig. $p = .053$); and (b) the most insignificant response came during the question "Does the Encore staff care about you?" (Sig. $p = .893$). With twelve-year-olds ($n = 14$) and thirteen-year-olds ($n = 22$), the variation in reporting was affected by the small sample size. Note that one 12-year-old did not respond to these questions, but 14 of 15 12-year-olds did respond.[48]

4.6 Discussion

4.6.1 Limitations

One limitation of this research included my lack of experience in administering an anonymous mixed-methods (qualitative and quantitative) survey. Second, while the evidence speaks for itself, it was not clear if a pretest/posttest format might have enhanced the reliability and validity of the data. I could only administer the survey as a single time-point test.

Another limitation was the decreased variation in the independent variable or control. The Jesuit-Sponsored School is an all-boys middle school, with 93 percent of its student composition African American. Moreover, with 79 percent of the Jesuit-Sponsored School students qualifying for the Federal/State Free and Reduced Lunch Program, the entire student body does not pay for breakfast, lunch, or snack. Thirty-five different zip codes comprised the Jesuit-Sponsored School student body. Statistically, it was difficult to analyze concepts without much variation; programmatically (*en vivo*, which means in real life), these similarities may have influenced the way that students viewed the program. It was not possible to detect the size of that influence from this evaluation.

After I administered my survey, the Jesuit-Sponsored School dismissed two students—one for poor attendance, the other for behavior. Of the fifty-seven total students attending the Jesuit-Sponsored School on March 12, 2009, fifty-five students completed the anonymous survey. Two sixth grade students were absent from school the day the survey was administered.

4.6.2 Implications

In Section III of the survey, students were asked about their personal goals and abilities. Students at the Jesuit-Sponsored School had a positive sense of self and valued the education they received from faculty and staff. Their responses suggested that the Jesuit-Sponsored School was helping support student growth as well as their interest in learning. At this school, 94.7 percent of students in Grades 7 through 8 believed they could do most things if they tried, while only 7 percent thought seriously about dropping out of school. No students answered "No" to questions about their abilities to do most things and if they did many things well. No students reported that they did not have goals and plans for the future. That students valued their education from the Jesuit-Sponsored School indicated that the school was promoting a sense of belonging to the school community—the goal of the *IPP* and a characteristic of a Jesuit-sponsored education. Students also reported, qualitatively, that the Jesuit-Sponsored School was highly regarded in the community and helped students attend the better private high schools. The Jesuit-Sponsored School Afterschool Program of Character Formation was helping students to attend school more often, thus directly promoting their flourishing.

In Section IV of the survey, students were asked about how they felt about the Jesuit-Sponsored School's Afterschool Program of Character Formation. Student responses suggested that this school program was providing students with physical and psychological safety, a sense of autonomy, and an opportunity to build creative skills. Students were less convinced that the Afterschool Program of Character Formation exposed them to things they could not normally do from home or in their community. While the Afterschool Program of Character Formation provided students with a safe environment, it was less clear if it affected academic performance.

The Afterschool Program of Character Formation was helping students to develop social skills and improve social-emotional intelligence; as students interacted with other students with whom they may not have gotten along, they did things to be helpful. In Section V of the survey, students were asked about the activities in the Jesuit-Sponsored School's Afterschool Program of Character Formation. It was clear that students should engage in the democratic process of making rules with each afterschool instructor, thereby increasing students' sense of ownership and self-determination. While the Afterschool Program of Character Formation exposed students to different physical and cognitive learning environments, the range of programming might be reviewed to increase student interest in activities. Students responding to qualitative questions reported "happiness" in attending the Afterschool Program of Character Formation, while others desired new programming like boxing and rap classes. Such responses indicated that the Afterschool Program of Character Formation might need to be reviewed for cultural responsiveness.

According to my results, as student age increased, a greater percentage of students reported improved self-esteem. This may evidence the success of the Afterschool Program of Character Formation; that is, as students spent more time in the program, their self-esteem increased. More testing will ensure that such results are statistically significant when controlling for other factors.

Section VI of the survey assessed the amount of time students spent on school-related subject matter as well as their prayer life. Students were doing their homework during study hall but reported spending "most" of their time on sports activities during afterschool hours. The finding that the Afterschool Program of Character Formation was also helping students to develop a prayer life was curious, as public schools neglect this point given concerns about the separation of church and state, privacy, and freedom of expression. The findings particularly suggest a greater sense of religiosity or spirituality among younger (age eleven) students in the Jesuit-Sponsored School's sixth grade.

A strong relationship between the Jesuit-Sponsored School Afterschool Program of Character Formation and students doing better academically could not be affirmed. The program was helping students to avoid fights and increase communication skills between peers; however, the sense of connection between grades and ages of students implied a sense of brotherhood.

4.6.3 Recommendations

At the beginning of each academic year, the Jesuit-Sponsored School Afterschool Program of Character Formation must be clearly defined for students and their parent(s)/guardian(s). Furthermore, the Jesuit-Sponsored School *Student and Family Handbook* must establish distinctive goals and objectives for the program. While students were self-reporting positive influences of the Afterschool Program of Character Formation, it was unclear if they felt the program's activities might be taken away if they did not answer questions in a certain way. Future studies should take into consideration the pretest/posttest model. The survey should be administered once at the beginning of the academic school year and for a final time at the end of the academic school year.

Periodically, the Jesuit-Sponsored School reviews its normal school day curriculum. An additional recommendation includes more professional development of the Afterschool Program of Character Formation pedagogy, especially discerning its relationship to and with the use of the *Ignatian Pedagogical Paradigm*. The administration should also develop profiles of the Ignatian Educator and Ignatian Staff Member, which is common at the Jesuit-Sponsored Schools.[49] The Afterschool Program of Character Formation should continue to be built into the school day and bridge the school day as it is currently formatted. The benefits students receive from the program come through its unity as well as the students' sense of belonging, self-determination, and autonomy.

Future analyses should look at the relationship between academic performance and time spent in study hall during the Encore Program. It is unclear just how students on Academic and Behavioral Probation receive the Afterschool Program of Character Formation; future studies might use these students as focus groups or control groups. Future studies might also look at budgetary information and the influence/impact that volunteer staff versus traditional staff have on the student body at the Jesuit-Sponsored School.

Additional studies should look at how qualitative responses indicate tensions between students who are perceived as outcasts and tensions among peer groups and among students with a lesser sense of community belonging. What are these students saying versus students who clearly perceive the value of the Jesuit-Sponsored School's Afterschool Program of Character Formation? Outcomes could lead to referrals to school-based or community-based organizations that deliver individual and family therapy. Researchers might ask: How do these students know that the Jesuit-Sponsored School is both preparing them for and will help them get into the best high schools?

4.7 Conclusion

Qualitative and quantitative research is key to evaluating afterschool education programs because they are tenets of evidence-based practice. Both types of research support evidence-based social work practice. As the Jesuit-Sponsored School develops and strengthens its school-wide curriculum, maturing over twenty plus years of development, an ongoing recommendation is that the Encore Afterschool Education and Enrichment Program be more formally organized and structured around the *IPP* and its concomitant educational and pedagogical goals and objectives. By integrating roles and identity, validation and promotion, a sense of belonging and autonomy/self-determination, youth can learn to love to learn and have fun while learning. Youth and youth outcomes are strongly tied to the organizations that support them. The more unified the school day and the more culturally competent the educational approach and afterschool intervention, then the stronger our children become. Such is the relationship between ecology and systems theory.[50] The Jesuit-Sponsored School succeeded in this because of its emphasis on delivering a quality Jesuit-sponsored education to students.

The Jesuit-Sponsored School's Afterschool Program of Character Formation must continue to meet the needs of students and their families, while also remaining dedicated to the mission and philosophy of a Jesuit Nativity Miguel Partner School. The Jesuit-Sponsored School should forever be mindful of its commitment "to serving young men who will in turn be committed to serving others: to the greater glory of God."[51]

In the next chapter, we journey with Ignatius to a New York City Public School. There, as in all NYC DOE schools, students receiving special education and related services are evaluated for placement in the Least Restrictive Environment (LRE) from the Most Restrictive Environment (MRE). I show how this in and of itself can be considered an application of the *Ignatian Pedagogical Paradigm*.

5

Special Education Placement (From Most Restrictive Environment to Least Restrictive Environment)

An Application of Ignatian Pedagogy and the *IPP* in a New York City Public School[1]

5.1 Introduction

At the New York City Public School (herein anonymized), where I worked as a school-based support team school social worker, 31 percent of the student population received special education (e.g., placement in a self-contained classroom) and related services (e.g., occupational therapy) through the implementation of an Individualized Education Plan (IEP) during the 2019–20 school year. In 2018, the New York City Public School was identified by the New York City Department of Education (NYC DOE) as a "spotlight school," which meant that the school was referring too many students for initial special education evaluations. In addition, the NYC DOE School Quality Guide 2018–19 reflected that the percentage of students with disabilities (SWDs) was comparatively higher than that of our peer schools in the district and city. This also meant that the movement of children from the Most Restrictive Environment (MRE) to the Least Restrictive Environment (LRE) was being monitored closely by district staff.

During the 2019–20 academic year, my colleagues and I decided to investigate this topic by determining the impact of appropriately moving five students (based on evidence and data about each student's academic, behavioral and social-emotional progress) from MRE to LRE within their school community. To protect the students, I anonymized them and changed their initials; the students studied were BR, CL, TT, RM, and DH. As I started to reflect on the project, I imagined both LRE movements and the *Ignatian Pedagogical Paradigm* (*IPP*) working synchronously to enhance a student's sense of community belonging, improve their mastery of educational content, grow their personal independence, and raise their awareness of gratitude. Neither special education nor faith in education should intentionally or unintentionally impinge on a student's ability to flourish in the classroom. In completing this pilot study, I envisioned a direct relationship between our goal of LRE and the *IPP*. Such a relationship would suggest that both the *IPP* and a program of character formation based on Ignatian Pedagogy for students and staff could be beneficial to NYC public schools. To prepare public students for future success, assumptions must be challenged.

5.2 The New York City Public School: General Demographics and Place of Practice

The New York City Public School, whose school motto is *Earn, Learn, Achieve, and Believe*, is located in an urban school district that is ethnically diverse. This learning community in the school is represented by more than twenty-five countries speaking more than ten languages. Eleven percent of the student population were English Language Learners (ELLs) or "multilingual learners." As of the 2020–1 school year, 30 percent of the school population were students with learning disabilities; they were eligible to receive special education with a classification like Autism or Other Health Impairment. High standards are set in all classrooms, with the goal of having students receive differentiated and specific instruction that is unique to each student's needs in a supportive learning environment. As per the 2018–19 NYC DOE School Quality Guide, the New York City Public School exceeded the citywide average in Common Core shifts in literacy and math, quality of student discussion, inclusive instructional practices, professional development, school commitment, safety, and social-emotional learning, for example, Respect for All. The parent coordinator (PC), in unison with the parents of the Parent Association (PA), provides workshops and other parent/guardian activities to increase parent/guardian involvement and to build capacity for parent engagement in the school (e.g., through programming with partners like a food program and a chorale program) and increase parent/guardian understanding and awareness of curriculum, such as the Teachers College Reading and Writing Project, Common Core Standards/New York Next Generation Learning Standards, test sophistication, and social and emotional needs of students in a post-Covid-19 world.

Staff at the New York City Public School are responsible for playing an active, positive, and supportive leadership role in the development and implementation of maintaining educational settings in the LRE for students. The planning and implementation of instruction is meaningful and involves the entire school staff. At the New York City Public School, the sense of community helps to foster self-esteem, pride in individual accomplishments, mutual respect, and a sense of belonging and self-worth among all students. One could argue that the New York City Public School features, implicitly, in its curriculum aspects of Ignatian Pedagogy, specifically the *Ignatian Pedagogical Paradigm:* contextual learning, experience, reflection, action, and evaluation, as well as characteristics of a Jesuit education, for example, creating men and women for others, to educate the "whole person, head and heart and intellect and feelings," according to Kolvenbach.[2]

As discussed earlier, Ignatian Pedagogy and the *IPP* suggest that, regardless of educational placement (special education or general education), students are accepted and supported by their peers and other members of the school community while their educational needs are being met. As a member of the staff, I frequently observed my colleagues to foster natural support networks so that students' social and emotional needs were being met—for example, when the special education placement/program was changed for a student who met his IEP goals. At the New York City Public School, staff supports the implementation of strategies from social-emotional programs, such as Sanford Harmony, and RULER (from the Yale Center for Emotional Intelligence), from social-emotional screeners, like the Devereux Student Strengths Assessment (DESSA), and the placement of outside agencies, such as a community-based organization, a mental health agency servicing students and parents through individual and family therapy, and a dance troupe within the school building to address community-based needs for afterschool programming.

Whether we are discussing Jesuit-Sponsored Schools or public schools in the NYC DOE, both general and special education students learn best in the mainstream environment of school and community life. It is believed that an inclusive environment strengthens the classroom and the students' sense of belonging and offers all of its members a greater opportunity for learning. Some of the benefits of the LRE include better preparation for adult life, better education, improved social skills, and higher expectations, all to benefit each student's academic and social-emotional well-being. All of these benefits result in more independence and success during elementary school and even after children with disabilities transition from middle school to high school and beyond.

5.3 Presupposition

In 2019, members of the administration and staff at the New York City Public School, including myself, raised concerns about special education placement recommendations based on feedback from the District office. A closer look at the quantifiable data revealed that a disproportionate percentage of students with disabilities engaged the curriculum in classrooms at the New York City Public School. Table 5.1 indicates the percentage of students having a disability classification at the New York City Public School, compared to the District and NYC. This table represents the special education population at the New York City Public School, referral rate, LRE recommendations, and SWDs with a paraprofessional from 2014–15 through 2018–19. For those unfamiliar with Special Education System of Supports it is abbreviated in the table as SETSS.

Together, we decided to investigate program recommendations for students with disability classifications. To complete the project, our team collected qualitative and quantitative data by administering surveys, analyzing students' English Language Arts (ELA) and Math performance, interviewing parents, and formally observing students in their classroom environment. We did this to assess and evaluate the academic success and social-emotional growth of students who, having achieved most of their IEP goals, could be re-evaluated and appropriately moved/placed (based on evidence and data about each student's academic, behavioral and social-emotional progress) from the NYC DOE School's more restrictive 12:1:1 (self-contained) classes to the less restrictive Integrated Co-Teaching (ICT) classes. Upon reflection, I observed that the impact of the transitions and, later, sustained moves revealed that certain students who

Table 5.1 Special Education Practice (as of May 31, 2019)

Percentage of Students with IEPs	MRE Recommendations Overall
2014–15 22.1%	From 2014–15 through 2018–19
2015–16 24.8%	ICT 59.6%
2016–17 23.6%	Small Class 36.2%
2017–18 28.7%	SETSS 1.1%
2018–19 28.5%	
Referral Rate Percentage	Percentage of SWDs with Paraprofessionals
2014–2015 4.1%	2014–15 6.2%
2015–16 6.1%	2015–16 7.5%
2016–17 4.7%	2016–17 9.4%
2017–18 7.7%	2017–18 10.6%
2018–19 3.1%	2018–19 16.9%

had been in self-contained classes actually flourished in the larger classroom environments; moreover, these students prospered even when challenged by a more rigorous academic curriculum and demonstrated resilience, despite social challenges due to their character formation and self-efficacy.

Such a result can be viewed through the lens of the Ignatian Pedagogy and the *IPP*—namely, that situational context led to reflection about a programmatic deficit, then to action to resolve the problem. Through the lens of the foundational facts and principles of the characteristics of a Jesuit education—namely, *cura personalis*, unity of heart, mind, and soul—students at the New York City Public School would then be further formed, with the goal of creating agents of change. Here, the idea of indifference can be applied; for example, Ignatius of Loyola spoke about indifference (a state of being impartial or unbiased) in terms of one's primary objective, to serve God.[3] In our case, as a team, we were free from disordered inclinations because our aim was the improved functioning of our students in their learning environment. While certain staff focused on theories of inclusive classrooms and school leadership, I focused on the implications of Ignatian Pedagogy and the *IPP* as they related to this specific pilot study and my research question.

Together, we met and discussed the school and classroom climate and culture, as well as the pedagogy and curriculum of the various MRE special education settings in our school. We determined that placement was not a setting for a child's entire educational career and that LRE is a principle that guides the appropriate placement of the student based on their IEP. Generally, the intent of LRE is to make sure that kids who receive special education services are included in the general education classroom as often as possible. Again, this is a direct link to the pedagogical philosophy of Ignatius of Loyola: the interaction of experience, reflection, and action, in this instance, specifically to liberate students with disabilities toward the end goal, which is to validate each student's experience in his or her learning environment.[4]

On a macro level, school program recommendations were reviewed to determine if students benefited from an MRE. As a result, we noticed that academic achievement was stagnant and wondered: If/when students move from an MRE to an LRE, will they benefit academically, behaviorally, and social-emotionally? As discussed in Chapter 3, a feminist interpretation of pedagogy liberates us to consider the effects on LRE moves on the student's experience of himself, herself, or theirself in relation to self, to others and, when part of the student's life, to God, or to a Higher Power. Again, education is not neutral; to limit students from accessing their faith or even their spirituality during the school day is not what is meant by the separation of church and state. Therein, the presumption is that public school education is free of catechesis or religious instruction.

5.4 The Recommended Special Education Program (12:1:1/ICT) Impacting Human Flourishing

Next, we discerned this focus question: How does the recommended special education program (ICT and 12:1:1) impact academic achievement? In terms of character formation and human flourishing, academic achievement is essential for human flourishing. Therefore, as a school, while we were showing growth and proficiency gains in academic performance, our self-contained student special education population was performing far below all of the other subgroups of students. Data from November of 2019 was analyzed, which indicated that the self-contained student population had a 1.67 average proficiency on both the New York State English Language Arts (NYS ELA) and Math (NYS Math) exams—far below the school's overall average proficiency of 2.73 in NYS ELA and the school's overall average proficiency of 2.93 in NYS Math. Additionally, as displayed in Table 5.1, during the 2018–19 school year, our special education population represented 28.5 percent of the total population, of which 59.6 percent of the IEP students were in an ICT class, and 36.2 percent of the IEP population were in a self-contained 12:1:1 class.

5.5 Discussion

For us to monitor student progress, an analysis of benchmark data was useful, including a review of IEPs and the writing of quality of IEPs; IEP goal attainment; Measure of Student Learning (MoSL); Teachers College Reading and Writing Project (TCRWP); Running Records; i-Ready; NYSAA (if applicable); ELL Periodic Assessments; NYS ELA and Math Assessments; and writing samples and as a result classroom assessments informed the development of Tier 2 and Tier 3 intervention groups for instruction, enrichment, and intervention.

As such, there was a direct link between academic success and student flourishing. The Blueprint for Improved Results for Students with Disabilities published by the New York State Education Department[5] highlights effective principles for supporting students with special needs. The document addresses how districts, schools, teachers, parents/guardians, and the students themselves play a vital role in determining flourishing or achievement/success in school. Of course, Ignatian Pedagogy, being far older already, emphasizes that students need to be supported in becoming self-advocates and learn how to set educational goals for themselves. It is essential that teachers provide evidence-based strategies, multiple entry points to instructional lessons, and explicit instruction in academic, behavioral and social-emotional learning. Other critical components which promote student success are effective systemic support, parental support, professional development for staff and teachers, high expectations set for students, and hiring staff to support and deliver the mission, vision, and goals of the school.

In *Creating an Inclusive School*, Richard Villa and Jacqueline Thousand explain the progression of special education law in the United States and the various interpretations of federal law.[6] Educators should be aware that special education has evolved over the past forty-five years. When federal law mandates that a student with a disability should only be removed from a general education setting when he/she has "failed to achieve satisfactorily" despite support(s), most schools respond by physically placing the student with a disability in a general education classroom for part of the school day without an explicit support plan. This sets students up for immediate failure and does not take into account a student's personal human flourishing.

After reviewing additional literature, we compared the academic standing of those children in the New York City Public School who were placed in a 12:1:1 class setting to those already sitting in an ICT setting to ensure that our school was promoting an inclusive environment. We observed the instruction in the 12:1:1 setting (multiage classrooms segmented into Grades K-1, 2-4 and 4-5), which revealed a tendency by the pedagogue to instruct the class through a "middle of the road" approach. The "middle of the road" approach is defined as teachers meeting their entire student body at a median between lowest and highest academic capability. Certainly, in my mind, this could be considered *Magis*, but it also suggested that the pedagogue asked questions about their students' involvement in the curriculum, content, and the personal meaning the students ascribed to their learning. Thus, while the *IPP* is not a method of teaching, it is curriculum design purposed toward implementing teaching values; it has been in use since 1993 and studied often by the International Commission on Apostolate of Jesuit Education (Society of Jesus).

In addition to reviewing the academic standing of the identified students, we examined the social-emotional impact of a 12:1:1 setting, compared to an ICT setting. We evaluated what students were exposed to in their 12:1:1 setting and compared it to what they were exposed to in their new ICT setting.

In keeping with my investigation of the utility of using Ignatian Pedagogy and the *IPP* in public schools, the pilot study indicated that to promote student flourishing within the context of moving students from MRE to LRE at the New York City Public School, staff should: (a) identify and meet the Pre-Kindergarten Turning-5 (T5) students placed through a Re-Evaluation of the Pre-K IEP in the 12:1:1 Kindergarten setting by their School-Based Support Teams in September, for example, to immediately evaluate the appropriateness of that recommendation based on the already existing composition of the 12:1:1 classroom setting; and (b) identify students in the 12:1:1 setting in June of the prior school year, for example, to reflect on the appropriateness of considering their movement from the 12:1:1 to the ICT setting during the upcoming academic year. Lessons learned were evaluated; thus, by tailoring and adjusting the pilot study, future students' academic and social-emotional well-being needs will be met, and students will be appropriately moved (based on evidence and data about each student's academic, behavioral, and social-emotional progress) from the 12:1:1 classroom setting to the ICT classroom setting. The relationship between these ideas and Ignatian Pedagogy and the *IPP* is further discussed in Chapter 6.

In sum, a best-practice recommendation is for when staff implements surveys in the future. Surveys should account for the established relationships between special education students and their related service providers; this is in direct opposition to Ignatian Pedagogy, which emphasizes the direct relationship between the teacher and the student. In the future, the surveys will include related service providers in the administration and analysis of the surveys. Related service providers at the New York City Public School generally service the same students throughout their enrollment at our school. Thus, such related service providers have more nuanced feedback regarding these special education students, for example, those who are being considered for movement from the MRE to the LRE.

A second conclusion raised concerns about the citywide NYC DOE Turning-5 process, which attempts to place Pre-K students appropriately in a Kindergarten class, based on their needs for special education and related services, but does not account for the "middle of the road" pedagogical approach of the preexisting 12:1:1 teacher/classroom, which may be a K-2 Grade bridge class. Students who enter their 12:1:1 classroom above their peers may not be challenged and find themselves bored; again, this is not *Magis*. This perhaps suggests a limitation of trying to universalize, for example, a program of character formation within the NYC DOE—specifically, who will monitor the implementation of best practices?

In Jesuit-Sponsored Schools, there is a frequent review of curriculum and program evaluation, but how would this be done effectively in such a large, urban education system? This is why the Jesuit-Sponsored Schools employ faculty directors of Ignatian Formation and vice presidents of mission, whose primary tasks are to ensure that the school is successfully and effectively implementing a characteristic Jesuit education, based on the tenets of Ignatian Pedagogy and the *IPP* to students.

5.6 General Application: Challenges and Growth

As a result of this pilot study, the following challenges and growth mindset points occurred.

As Pre-K students are evaluated through the Turning-5 (T5) process, School Psychologists and School Social Workers should meet with parents and observe future zoned community school students in their Pre-K classroom setting. During this process, parents are educated about program offerings in the zoned community school and learn about how their child or children fit into the NYC DOE Kindergarten program, targeting academic success, a sense of community belonging, and the human flourishing of the student through a program in character formation. A large proportion of T5 parents seek to place their children in "smaller classroom settings," believing in a misnomer: that a smaller class size means LRE. In fact, a smaller class does not necessarily mean LRE.

After the school psychologist and/or school social worker clarifies the size of average NYC DOE classrooms to the parents, the parents become more knowledgeable about LRE and MRE class sizes. As a consequence, they grow more open to discussing and discerning the appropriate placement recommendation (based on evidence and data about each student's academic, behavioral and social-emotional progress) for their child or children; here, the parents experience a combination of freedom and indifference, as well as capacity building for greater participation in their child's life at school. At this point, it is important for the school's principal to meet with the School-Based Support Team in anticipation of and about the pending T5 IEP meeting with the parent/guardian. A first question is: If the school principal guides the process toward most appropriately placing the T5 child into the community school, how might they form their staff to deliver *cura personalis* or establish the framework for use of Ignatian Pedagogy and the *IPP* in their school?

The goal of T5 placement is to place students in the LRE where they will be challenged to learn and flourish as members of the school community, thus accounting for *cura personalis* and the relationship between the person and the school community, *cura apostolica*. A second question is: How will the school principal educate the pedagogical staff and help them learn about New York State's expectations and laws surrounding students with disabilities as related to the delivery of special education and related services, for example, Family Educational Rights and Privacy Act (FERPA, 1974), Individuals with Disabilities Act (IDEA, 1975), Americans with Disabilities Act (ADA, 1990), and No Child Left Behind Act (NCLB, 2002). This is important because the pedagogical staff are key stakeholders—those staff who work directly with the students and their parents to implement the curriculum.

With regard to this pilot study, the principal at the New York City Public School held a two-day staff training on the New York State and United States of America Federal Law, as described by the Blueprint for Improved Results for Students with Disabilities, where faculty, staff, and the administration explored and reviewed the principal's vision, the school's mission, and the goals for delivering the principal's educational philosophy, for example, how it would be implemented over the coming months and years. Finally, as part of the pilot study, faculty were surveyed to gain insight into their new understanding about LRE placement, and again, I analyzed that data to evaluate correspondence with the tenets of Ignatian Pedagogy and the *IPP*.

A similar program was offered to family workers and related service providers (speech and language therapist, occupational therapist, physical therapist, and school psychologist). By doing this, all staff were informed about the New York City Public School's movement toward LRE for SWDs, for example, about educating students with disabilities, and about how an inappropriate placement could affect a student's flourishing.

Finally, this pilot study provided me with an opportunity to see, directly and indirectly, how a public school might be able to implement Ignatian Pedagogy, the *IPP*, and a program of character formation based on the characteristics and framework of a Jesuit education.

5.7 Looking Toward Ignatian Pedagogy and the *Ignatian Pedagogical Paradigm*

To examine the benefit of the pilot study, staff, including teachers, paraprofessionals, and related service providers, were asked to complete exit tickets. The qualitative analysis of the exit tickets led to feedback regarding how staff understood the direction toward LRE placement and the vision of school leadership at the New York City Public School. The staff responses demonstrated how LRE placement affected the wider New York City Public School community and culture. Here, it is important to note that Jesuits like Fr. Dean Brackley have served in places like Latin America, and his experiences have shaped his thinking and experience. The same can be said for staff who work through, in, and from their local culture, school environment, and neighborhood. Staff at the New York City Public School understood LRE placement and school leadership at the New York City Public School in the following manner (the parallel characteristic of a Jesuit education is listed in parentheses):

Leadership: Effective and Supportive (Men and Women for Others)

Staff at the New York City Public School understood the implementation of IDEA and other educational law as benefiting the school community, noting that in many ways staff and students were being formed to be in direct relationship with self and others.

Students: Self-Advocacy and Self-Efficacy (*Cura Personalis* and Forming and Educating Agents of Change)

The students at the New York City Public School were increasingly being challenged to advocate for their own needs, and to have, as the educator Kathy Kolbe suggested, belief in their own innate abilities, strengths, including cognitive strengths.[7]

Parents: Involvement and Empowerment (Unity of Heart, Mind, and Soul)

Parents are said to be involved and empowered to participate in their students' curriculum while they are enrolled at the New York City Public School.

School: Environment/Culture and Differentiated Instruction (Forming and Educating Agents of Change, *Magis*)

The New York City Public School presents itself as a school with an environment/culture driven by specific and differentiated instruction, as well as the creation of quality IEPs.

5.8 Discerning the Evidence of Impact

The teachers at the New York City Public School reflected on the principles of LRE and engaged in group conversations to reflect and discern best practices for serving and reaching SWDs at the New York City Public School.

Teachers at the New York City Public School reported that a school-wide improvement plan, beyond what was already defined by the school's Consolidated Plan and the Comprehensive Education Plan could be created toward the end of implementing/targeting Multi-Tiered System of Supports (MTSS) (formerly Response to Intervention [RTI]) for student's academic success and improvement, behavioral management, and social-emotional growth and well-being. The teachers imagined the benefits of collaboration and team meetings between special education teachers and related service providers as essential to delivering mandated special education services.

Teachers at the New York City Public School saw the need for additional (new) academic programming to promote student independence and self-advocacy, all in keeping with the spirit of Ignatian Pedagogy, for example, the teacher and the student are co-learners, even at times, co-teachers. Some special education students at the New York City Public School, relied too much on the teachers to tell them what to do—hence, the need for character formation to improve student efficacy and agency. Thus, I ask: If you believe in the growth mindset and inclusive classrooms, how does this translate into the classroom over time, albeit if not overnight? One method useful for delivering this is implementing the *IPP* and a program of character formation based on Ignatian Pedagogy in public schools.

5.9 Conclusion

What if students could be agents of their own learning process and there was no limit to where learning ends in school and begins at home? Students have much to learn, but so do their family members. Human beings can never stop learning. What about transforming schools through a curriculum based on "real life"— that is, by developing a program where learning is collaborative, creates a more positive learning environment, and fosters the connection between the school, the family, and the wider community?

As a result of this pilot study, the school successfully and appropriately (based on evidence and data about each student's academic, behavioral and social-emotional progress) integrated the five 12:1:1 students (BR, CL, TT, RM, and DH) into an ICT setting during the 2019–20 school year. In doing so, the ICT classroom environment was strengthened and thereby offered all of its students many greater opportunities for learning. For the 2020–1 school year, these five students will continue in the LRE. Those moving to middle school were prepared for their transition through exit interviews and a review of their future cycles of learning/education program in the middle school. For all five students (BR, CL, TT, RM, and DH), as identified through administered interviews, this move provided them with a better quality of education, improved social skills, and higher expectations of self beyond mere superficiality.

Our journey with Ignatius has led us to this question: What can the public schools within and without the NYC DOE learn from Ignatian Pedagogy and the *IPP* as well as the characteristics of a Jesuit education? What is the benefit to public schools when universal programs of character formation based on context, experience, reflection, action, and evaluation are incorporated citywide? What are the concomitant results, consolations, and desolation? Such implications are discussed in Chapter 6.

6

Ignatian Pedagogy and the *Ignatian Pedagogical Paradigm*

Implications and Findings for New York City Public Schools

6.1 Implications and Findings

Secularism, the state of separation from religious institutions, and atheism, the idea that God does not exist, contend that happiness is not linked to God (Whom they deny exists), and that material possessions (obtained through the free market and/or capitalism) are the sine qua non of happiness.[1] Others who do not practice religion say that secularism and atheism are sufficient for living the good life, for example, happiness, in a way that is not linked to God, Whom they deny exists.[2] Perhaps such people have cautioned against God-speak in schools, holding the balance of the separation of church and state and liberalism and urban public education in their hands. Yet, such a balance can be revisited through the hermeneutical lens of Ignatian Pedagogy, the *IPP*, and its application to NYC DOE public schools.

Nowadays in schools, everybody tends to work in a silo, confined to their own space(s); they rarely collaborate with others due to a lack of resources and the traditional grammar of schooling.[3] Together, it is easier to solve the issues; we need to humanize the education experience by creating an educational experience centered on community voices. By implementing the best practices of Ignatian Pedagogy, public schools can become stronger communities of learners that engages families in an effort to work together toward an end—the cultivation of community voices. As González et al. (2006) discussed in their seminal work *Funds of Knowledge: Theorizing Practice in Household*, bringing the home into the traditional school improves children's both academic and socioemotional skills.[4] However, most urban public schools, even when designated a Community School, lack the capacity to forge a meaningful connection with families.

As discussed in Chapter 1, Ignatius of Loyola's experience of God led to greater freedom; hence, he organized his First Principle and Foundation in his *Spiritual Exercises* to reflect his lived reality of freedom and indifference.[5] Yet, such freedom and indifference are not tools or instruments of catechesis in either Ignatian Spirituality; they are about striving to live one's life unselfishly with a mind toward the other, toward becoming a man or woman for others, which translates to tenets of the characteristics of a Jesuit education. As stated earlier, the foundational question in my project is: Can the pedagogical philosophy of Ignatius of Loyola, as employed through Ignatian Pedagogy and the *Ignatian Pedagogical Paradigm*, lead the NYC DOE to: (a) develop a universal program of character formation and (b) improve the human flourishing of public school students by offering students an educational program based on human relationships and the acquisition of knowledge? The short answer is yes. Both pilot studies at the Jesuit-Sponsored School and the New York City Public School suggest ways in which Ignatian Pedagogy and the *IPP* serve the Jesuit-Sponsored School students (through an afterschool program in character formation) and NYC DOE students (academic achievement, behavioral growth, and social-emotional well-being through moving students with disabilities from MRE to LRE classroom settings) to promote human flourishing through, for example, emphasizing *cura personalis*.

Through the pilot studies, I was able to examine the social interactions, behaviors, and perceptions of the students being directly exposed to Ignatian Pedagogy in the Jesuit-Sponsored School's Afterschool Program of Character Formation, and indirectly at the New York City Public School through the placement of five students (anonymized as BR, CL, TT, RM, and DH) in the LRE learning environment. This research helped me refine *my preliminary and working definition of an emancipatory feminist theory of human flourishing*: human flourishing (or happiness) is defined as the realization of one's human potential (*sic* capacity)—more specifically, the realization of one's basic human endowments—in a manner that suits and underscores the individual's uniqueness as well.[6] Happiness is not purely subjective; it should never be tied to pleasure or satisfaction for its own sake without considering the purpose of human beings.[7] Thus, a finding is that the *IPP* can promote human flourishing in the Jesuit-Sponsored Schools and public schools.

Ignatius of Loyola's system of education has lasted far longer than the public school system. There are meaningful ways in which the *IPP* can be applied in the public school setting, if not to effect Ignatius of Loyola's understanding that human beings flourish when in the right relationship with self and others and a higher power. I began my analysis by looking at Ignatius's pedagogical philosophy through the hermeneutic of the *IPP* and hypothesized how it might be applied in the public school system, leading to an analysis of my work at the New York City Public School, for example, through the movement of students from the MRE to the LRE (based on evidence and data about each student's academic, behavioral, and social-emotional progress). The next finding suggested that a public school is not charged with catechesis; as feminist theologians reminded us, faith and pedagogy can exist in synchronicity in that environment without violating the separation of church and state. From my own observations, I understand that Ignatius's pedagogy radically involves a thoroughgoing "self-overcoming" (mortification) and the pursuit of prudence, resulting in discreet charity and learning from tradition.[8] An implication is that, for Ignatius of Loyola, freedom and flourishing are intimately connected.[9] The centerpiece of Ignatian Spirituality is freedom from fear, inordinate attachments, desires vs. wants, freedom to love service, truth speaking, and the like. Thus, Ignatian Pedagogy and the *IPP* offer NYC DOE educators a new way to attempt in their classrooms a rigorous and provocative pedagogy that centers on contextual education and the relationship between the pedagogue(s) and the learner(s). It also introduces new ideas like days of service and service retreats into the year-long urban public school curriculum, and possibly the afterschool curriculum.

My pilot studies will, I hope, lead to further examination of the application of Ignatian Pedagogy and the *IPP* in other public school contexts, such as high school retreats that look to broaden the students' awareness of self in relationship to others. Such retreats will be contextual and allow for students to reflect on their lives within the context of the Black Lives Matter Movement, the #MeToo Movement, and the Covid-19 pandemic. Education plays an important role in shaping the beliefs and perspectives of people, which is why it is important for public schools, likely through a rebranding in the face of losing students to private schools and charter schools, to reimagine spaces where students can flourish in their zoned school and community learning environment.

6.2 Expanding the Discourse

The students who participated in both pilot studies benefited in different ways from exposure to features of Ignatius's pedagogical philosophy. This research was important to conduct because (a) public schools in NYC may be interested in adopting and implementing a universal program of character formation for students, and (b) the Ignatian Pedagogy provides a method of personal formation and discernment useful for developing public school students for life in the real world in the twenty-first century. I offer to readers the possibility that such programming in character formation may attract back to the NYC DOE those families who sought such programming from private schools and charter schools during the Covid-19 pandemic. About 2 percent of former NYC DOE students left the public education system since the start of the pandemic in 2020; that is approximately +/−64,000 students, while half of the city districts lost 10 percent of students since 2017, these numbers are trending up not down.[10] As noted already, the Ignatian Pedagogy provides a framework for forming the whole person (mind/body/soul); Ignatius's philosophy benefits the desires of educators who see their students struggling to make meaning of a complex and messy world—boys and girls, young women and men who desire to meet others in their struggle to be *people for others*, who seek *Magis* (Ignatius of Loyola's term for the depth of human relationship, or More—the More as discussed earlier in this book).

So what? Of course, my project is the first of its kind; a search for literature on the topic of Ignatian Pedagogy, the *IPP*, and public school system yielded few resources. To date, I found little analysis on the impact of exposure to Ignatian Pedagogy and the *IPP* on public school students; even academic work on Ignatian Spirituality and other religious denominations is dint, beyond the work of Paolo Gamberini at the University of San Francisco.[11] Therefore, Ignatius of Loyola offers the opportunity for public school administrators and faculty to engage a pedagogical philosophy in qualitative and quantitative research without worrying about a violation of the separation of church and state.

It is important to discuss Ignatian Pedagogy and its impact on student achievement, for example, human flourishing for public school students, because the findings may be broadly employed to develop programs of *character* formation in the NYC DOE, as well as a tool to improve enrollment in public schools across America. One of the main differences between large public school programs and their competitors—charter schools and private schools—is the offerings of programs in character formation, and that their graduates are expected to achieve a distinct profile upon graduation, for example, the Profile of the Grad (of Jesuit-Sponsored Schools) at Graduation.

6.3 Conclusion

My research on the application of Ignatian Pedagogy and the *IPP* in public schools in the NYC DOE suggested that it may be adopted without violating the separation of church and state. Ignatian Pedagogy and the *IPP* are not catechetical tools; they are instruments that lead students through context, experience, reflection, action, and evaluation to become citizens who are men and women for others; who practice the care of the whole person; who are united in heart, mind, and soul; who do things not for self but for others (and possibly a higher power); who become agents of change; and who strive always to do more good in the world.

Through my research, I also saw the need for/benefit of adult formation programs grounded in the pedagogy of Ignatius of Loyola. My initial hypothesis pointed to the basic fundamental fact that public schools, including students and staff, can benefit from programs of character formation based on Ignatian Pedagogy and the *IPP*. Schools would need to employ a Director of Formation, like a literacy coach, to ensure the successful delivery of programming, with the development and staff in alignment with the pedagogical methods of this paradigm. Such an employee can support the school's administration who principally hires staff to deliver the school's mission, vision, goals, and values. The Director of Formation can also monitor the progress of nontenured and tenured staff in delivering the pedagogical and character formation curriculum, for example, by running the school's professional development program for tenured and untenured staff.

My research is relevant to the wider discussion on character formation and human flourishing in the field of Ignatian Spirituality. Historically, Ignatius of Loyola tended to the close formation of religious communities—his own religious order (the Society of Jesus, the Jesuits), and communion rituals—he advocated for the frequent reception of Holy Communion. Ignatius of Loyola himself established many practices for deepening one's faith; his *Spiritual Exercises* are in many ways a methodology for growing and measuring the depth of the faithful and their corresponding lives lived in Jesus Christ.[12]

I completed this research because I was interested in the many ways Ignatian Pedagogy and the *IPP* develop a student's interior life and experience of human flourishing. Two questions I asked often during the completion of this project were: How would Ignatian Pedagogy and the *IPP* affect a public student's experience of self and others without violating the separation of church and state? and Can Ignatian Pedagogy and the *IPP* impact a public school student's experience of human flourishing (happiness) without being a direct form of evangelization or catechesis? It was important to ask these questions because I remain convinced that Ignatian Pedagogy and the *IPP* are useful as a method of character formation for students (and adults) that can be appropriately implemented in public schools like those in the NYC DOE.

From the literature reviewed on the *Ratio Studiorum*, Ignatian Pedagogy, and the *IPP*, I suggest that systems of public school education can learn much from the continuance of Jesuit education (e.g., as an exemplar par excellence). Public schools can form their students and emphasize cultural self-appropriation for the students, thus building a sense of community that transcends education. Public schools can offer a more structured sense of the progression of the curriculum, helping families to know more clearly when their children's formal education is complete. As Claude Pavur so rightly pointed out, "There is a guiding maxim, *Non multa, sed multum*: do not aim for coverage of vast amounts of content, but rather for depth in the appreciation and understanding of the material that is taken up."[13] It is our free public education that can learn much from the Humanist Tradition, allowing students to be fed on multiple levels—social-emotional, behavioral, spiritual, and intellectual. Faculty must see themselves as stakeholders, agents, and collaborators in a system of educational character formation, where the end result is the most cogent total formation of students (for the world) as possible.

Throughout this interdisciplinary work and journey with Ignatius of Loyola, I have provided readers and educators, especially those interested in public school and urban education, character formation programs, and the pedagogical philosophy of Ignatius of Loyola, with an opportunity to reflect about the synchronous relationship between public school education and Ignatian Pedagogy and the *IPP*. It is fair to say that many families are leaving the public school system, enrolling their children in private schools and charter schools today, even using taxpayer funding to offset costs through tuition assistance, as affirmed in the recent US Supreme Court ruling in *Carson v. Makin* (2022). By offering public schools the opportunity to create a universal program of character formation based on the tenets of Ignatian Pedagogy and the *IPP* and the characteristics of a Jesuit education, public schools can bridge the best practices of both worlds. It can be said, amid all the good found in public schools, that they are scrambling individually (due to underfunding, shortages in staffing, lack of attraction to the profession of education) and remain disconnected from each other; thus, they face a tremendous burden to form their students for the twenty-first century. Such public schools and school districts can resolve this problem by taking a closer look at the pedagogy of Ignatius of Loyola and Ignatian Pedagogy and by considering the *IPP* as a tool/method of instruction from which their students can flourish. Public school education and the character formation of its students can be considered the rationale for study, if not the pedagogical paradigm needed for students in the twenty-first century.

My interest in both society and the human character has shaped this project about character formation in public schools and the shared responsibility between all members of the educational community to form youth. I have selected a poem of great meaning by William Wordsworth titled "A Character" (written in 1800) to end this project. More than ever before, students and staff can be formed to be in the right relationship with self and others. We can, like Wordsworth suggested, steer students toward the heart of humanity, which is Agapetic Love. Wordsworth wrote:

> I marvel how Nature could ever find space
> For so many strange contrasts in one human face:
> There's thought and no thought, and there's paleness and bloom
> And bustle and sluggishness, pleasure and gloom.
>
> There's weakness, and strength both redundant and vain;
> Such strength as, if ever affliction and pain
> Could pierce through a temper that's soft to disease,
> Would be rational peace—a philosopher's ease.
>
> There's indifference, alike when he fails or succeeds,
> And attention full ten times as much as there needs;
> Pride where there's no envy, there's so much of joy;
> And mildness, and spirit both forward and coy.
>
> There's freedom, and sometimes a diffident stare
> Of shame scarcely seeming to know that she's there,
> There's virtue, the title it surely may claim,
> Yet wants heaven knows what to be worthy the name.
>
> This picture from nature may seem to depart,
> Yet the Man would at once run away with your heart;
> And I for five centuries right gladly would be
> Such an odd such a kind happy creature as he.

The final chapter introduces my framework for creating the Beloved Community. This framework is an essential meditation on and colloquy about the importance of taking seriously the need for creating and implementing a universal program of character formation in public schools based on the pedagogical philosophy of Ignatius of Loyola.

7

A Framework for Human Flourishing and the Creation of the Beloved Community

7.1 Introduction

I return to the question posed in the Introduction: Why does character formation in public schools matter? As a school social worker, I see human flourishing thwarted and impinged on by classism, prejudice, discrimination, acculturation, and stigma. Today, in the United States, factionalism, groupthink, and an ultraconservative Supreme Court are eroding the civil rights of a majority of citizens. This is why education of youth, pedagogy, curriculum, and character formation are essential: knowledge is power. In my tenure with the NYC DOE, I have met young men who are bullied because they are "gay" or "Black," young gay teenagers who may or may not be attracted to people of the same sex (or gender), and young Black youth whose self-esteem is affected by the White patriarchal norm. Marginalized youth, like all youth, long to be known for the human people they are—boys, girls, gender nonconforming, or BIPOC children of all shapes and sizes. They seek not to be judged because of who they love or because of the color of their skin, but rather because of who they are: God's beloved children, born in God's image and likeness. Such youth desire to contribute positively to the social world that often rejects them as immoral agents, thus making them unsafe outsiders and fringe characters (aka second-class citizens).

Time and time again, whether it was as a priest-in-training and guidance counselor in a Jesuit high school, or now as a layman and school social worker for the NYC DOE, I hear negative labels like "q*$$rr," "f@g," "h*&o," "g*^l," "p*$$y," "n#&&er," or "f*!^y"—all used by my school-age youth to reference the indiscriminate bullying of people who are effeminate, not-the-right-color, different, weird, and on and on.

More often than not, these youth are targets because they are empathic, sensitive, and altogether pensive about life; they reflect on life with only a mother at home or, perhaps, how their gay dads donate time, talent, and treasure to their local Roman Catholic Church but cannot "come out" publicly to their community of faith. Some stigmatizing and prejudicial children told some of my students "to die," "to kill themselves" because the world would be better off without them; they wrote them hateful, threatening messages on social media. These young men came or were brought to see the school social worker for a host of reasons but usually at a breaking point. Clearly, oppression is a learned process, and unfortunately may be ubiquitous due to time, circumstance, and scapegoating.

The Jewish philosopher and theologian Abraham Joshua Heschel reminded us, "The prophet does not see the world from the point of view of a political theory; he is a person who sees the world from the point of view of God; he sees the world through the eyes of God."[1] As the Psalmist knows, God is alive, and with the psalmist I sing: *My flesh and my heart may fail, but God is the rock of my heart, and my portion is forever. . . . The Lord is my shepherd; I shall not want.*[2] In this chapter, I provide a philosophical, social work, and theologically oriented framework for creating the Beloved Community. It demonstrates how I would dismantle oppression or, at the least, deconstruct the ideology perpetuating oppression. The objective of this final chapter of my text is to provide a comprehensive portrait of the characteristics and causes of oppression in the United States and the social, historical, and psychological systems that have allowed oppression to be perpetuated in our society.

I begin by asking the question: What is human flourishing?

As already defined in my book, human flourishing (or happiness, well-being) can be defined as the realization of one's human potential—more specifically, the realization of one's basic human endowments, in a manner that suits the individual's uniqueness as well.[3] The notion of human flourishing is useful for answering philosophical questions about what we ought to do or what sorts of human beings we should try to be, and clinical questions such as what sorts of lives we should hope for. Some theologians and social activists, like Mohandas K. Gandhi and Martin Luther King, Jr., sought to understand human flourishing within the context of doing the will of God or gods. Still, their projects were oriented beyond raising group consciousness and individuals' insight, toward mobilizing social activists. Such existential questions and social activism remain important today because certain individuals and groups find their flourishing frustrated as a result of social injustice, structural violence, evil, and so on. In the racialized socio-political context of the United States, race is a prominent social group category with attending structural and other forms of violence—thus, my decision to consider "race" as a social group category.

Consider the construct's perspectives of race and its relationship to racism.[4] Racism "is the belief that humans are subdivided into distinct hereditary groups that are innately different in their social behavior and mental capacities and that therefore can be ranked as superior or inferior."[5] Racism is both ethnocentric and a form of cultural imperialism. Social work researchers Flavio Marsigilia and Stephen Kulis reminded readers that "race has no basis in genetics or biology" and that socially constructed forms of oppression, marginalization, and exploitation exist to "target [individuals] and groups for discrimination."[6] Ethnic stratification systems also lead to differential treatment of minorities.[7] As a society, we can do more to eradicate hate and to promote human flourishing.

To start my personal inquiry about human flourishing, I place my discussion in the context of a globalizing, intersectional, culturally relevant, and interreligious world where: (a) instant access to information can spread (but also challenge) deep-seated labels, categories, and roles, for example, all homeless men are drug abusers; (b) new expectations about community life and life-span planning affect behaviors, boundaries, and skills, for example, the creation of virtual/online communities, especially during the Covid-19 pandemic, the elimination of national borders; and (c) economic and political systems invite and disinvite individuals and groups to participate in citizenship, thereby promoting unity or causing disunity, for example, the US government's expansion of the naturalization process for some undocumented immigrants versus the historically imperialistic advancements of American culture.

Even in our globalizing, intersectional, culturally relevant, and interreligious world, human life remains full of paradox, growing increasingly complex and messy.[8] (The tragedy of social sin remains alive and real; the presence of evil remains.) Mohandas K. Gandhi commented this way about the well-being of all when he stated:

> Man should earnestly desire the well-being of all God's creation and pray that he may have the strength to do so. In desiring the well-being of all lies his own welfare; he who desires only his own or his community's welfare is selfish and it can never be well with him.[9]

As a school social worker in the NYC DOE, I creatively and humanely respond to the messiness and surprises of human life, to the forces confronting soul-force and the strength of body, soul, and mind,[10] by being committed to individuals and groups whose human flourishing is thwarted, especially victims of structural violence and discrimination. As a school social worker and published author, I challenge society (nonviolently) through my writing to develop mutual recognition and respect (value) for all of its members, especially the individuals and groups affected by structural violence and discrimination, those who cannot rely on their inner selves for strength, courage, or hope.[11] Relying on the inner self is not enough for survival; structural change is due. In my specific case, I promote the full dignity and worth of LGBTQ+ people who are being fired from employment and volunteer activities by the Roman Catholic Church because of whom they love. The concept of intersectionality aptly frames how multidimensionality influences and impacts the degree of oppression an LGBTQ+ person may experience; for example, consider the "triple jeopardy" an African American lesbian may face with marginalization along three social group identities: gender, race, and sexuality.[12] Or consider my memoir, where I situated my departure from priestly training in the Society of Jesus due to the firing of lesbian and gay employees and volunteers by the Roman Catholic Church.[13] It is clear what happens when, as one example, a gay choir director is fired from a Roman Catholic Church because he is married to a man, or when a Jesuit-Sponsored School is stripped of its Catholic identity because it displays LGBTQ+ Pride and Black Lives Matter Flags. The impact on the person (the gay man and his family/friends), the organization (the local church), and the institution (the Roman Catholic Church) is profound. We can hope for change.

The nonviolent peace activists and prophets Mohandas K. Gandhi and Martin Luther King, Jr., commenced their testaments of hope by asking: What is the relationship between being children of God and human flourishing? For them, human flourishing was tied to doing the will of God or gods, especially by taking the moral high ground. Gandhi and King expressed God's love for humanity and taught society how to respect the dignity and worth of every human person. They did not fear death; they did not avoid pain or suffering to experience pleasure or happiness. They claimed truth and nonviolence as their cardinal virtues; such virtues reject classism, prejudice, mendacity, discrimination, acculturation, and stigma. Gandhi and King believed in a personal Godhead, one who created humanity in the Godhead's image and likeness, thereby emphasizing the dignity and worth of all human beings. To Gandhi and King, truth had to be followed at any cost. Today, the whole future of the United States still depends on their impact, their understanding of human flourishing.

My aim here in this final chapter is to demonstrate that Gandhi and King influence my conception of human flourishing and to find some common ground (holy ground) so that entrance into dialogue (pluralistically) can lead to the improvement of human flourishing and not the marginalization (or ostracism) of individuals or groups. In seeking to address the critical aspect of "causation," particular attention is made to these four content areas: human nature, epistemology, ethics, and the Philosophy of God and religion. In doing so, I demonstrate how oppression negates the dignity and worth of human beings while identifying how cultural imperialism marginalizes individuals because of their racial, ethnic, or cultural phenotype. My framework for human flourishing and the creation of the Beloved Community is a remedy for dismantling oppression as I have identified it in our society.

7.2 Human Nature

The concept of human flourishing and human good helps me explore the relationship between human nature, human individuality, and group membership; when seen together, this provides me with an opportunity to connect **the how:** a program of character formation in public schools, with **the what:** Ignatian Pedagogy, the *Ignatian Pedagogical Paradigm* (*IPP*), and human flourishing. Human flourishing is objective, individualized, diverse (flexible), self-directed, and social. Since human flourishing is dependent on who and what one is, it is important for me to articulate an account of human nature that is agent-/group-relative and open-ended. Thus, my appeal to understanding human flourishing starts with a discussion of human nature in general; this will bear greater fruit in my section on Ethics, where I discuss mutual recognition and respect. Remember, we are always in the process of becoming, never simply educated for the sake of acquiring knowledge, but rather to be formed to use that knowledge to improve the community.

7.2.1 Basic Human Endowments

Traditionally, human beings are regarded as having capacities for sensation, appetite, creativity, will, and intellect (which enables reflection). As an intellectual activity, reflection includes the implementation of reason: (a) to be self-critical and (b) to ask questions. From their capacity for intellect, human beings can thus form concepts freely and self-critically. Although vulnerable to our social environment and shaped by it, human beings do not just respond to stimuli but have a capacity to think and act autonomously, that is, on the basis of their own critical reflection. Human beings have feelings and intuition and can be spiritually connected to their existence. Consider how Gandhi and King experienced their worlds and responded to them by seeking transformative change, for example, eradicating stigma and conversion of hearts and minds and eliminating prejudice; both desired to create new nations with a people steeped in self-determination and self-rule (*Swaraj*).

At the same time, human flourishing is objectively tied to our nature as human beings, as creatures belonging to a species whose members are endowed with sense and intellect.[14] Every human being is unique, having individual differences, personal histories, and so on. As unique individuals, human beings develop their intellect, depending on where they find life. Some human beings become firefighters, others are accountants or social workers. In this way, individual human beings develop their intellectual capacity (general species capacity), for example, but in a way that satisfies more specific talents and inclinations. As such, a human being who is not talented in or inclined toward software design will likely be frustrated by a career in computer science, while another human being might find this same job exciting. Thus, human flourishing is objective, grounded, and self-directed—grounded in critical reflection and free choice. Of course, such anathemas to being, such as slavery or caste location and vulnerability to substance and alcohol use disorders, frustrate, thwart, and impinge on a person's or group's access to human flourishing.

To summarize: for a human being to flourish, he or she must pursue goals (freely) that are rational for *him or her individually* and not merely for him or her as a human being. Such rational and individual pursuit of goals depends on the implementation of reason, but in the awareness that each human being's species capacities can be realized in many ways. Individuals are endowed with different intellectual talents, have different particular interests, and so on.

Human beings are social animals; therefore, human flourishing also occurs in interpersonal relationships. Human beings enter into relationships with other human beings based on mental, biological, spiritual needs, and the like. Human beings also form relationships based on proximity and exposure to others, for example, students in public school, families in public housing, and college students at a university. Individual human beings are not wholly self-sufficient; rather, as social animals, human beings are dependent on other human beings. More specifically, human beings (a) enjoy particular bonds with other human beings (e.g., friendship); (b) need other human beings (e.g., for basic human needs; to develop the capacity of reason, intuition, and possibly prayer or spiritual experiences); and (c) acquire identity in and through human sociability (i.e., membership in a group). Unlike animals, human beings also have the capacity for higher culture (e.g., the creation of art). Culture presupposes the ability to create and sustain community.

7.2.2 The Human Family

The elementary group is the family; without the family, no society can develop. The family unit includes the human being's primary caregivers: the group one is born into and the group in which one acquires primary socialization. The human family is the first site for socialization—it is the first site where the individual learns his or her roles and other necessities.[15] Members of every family system must learn secure attachments as well as ways to relate to individuals and groups in society, including learning how to communicate, listen, and build relationships with other communicants.[16] Families transmit and translate virtues and vices, including good and bad behaviors and appropriate emotions, for their members. Martin Luther King, Jr., reflected that his own family was a place "where love was central and where lovely relationships were ever present."[17]

Human sociability is open-ended; individuals flourish differently. Just as the needs of individuals and groups evolve over time, so do the meanings and definitions associated with individuals and groups. Consequently, all family arrangements are unique and diverse. We can distinguish between traditional and nontraditional families. The "traditional family is defined as consisting of a husband (male), a wife (female) and their children, although this no longer is the predominant picture of family life in [the United States]."[18] Today, less than 30 percent of all families are considered traditional; traditional families are often referred to as the nuclear family.[19] By "non-traditional family system," I employ a personal definition of the family arrangement that does not meet the classical understanding of the traditional family, for example, a nontraditional family system might include two lesbians or two gay men, a single man or a single woman, for example, blended families. Nontraditional family systems may or may not include children. Some might even consider interracial families as part of the definition of nontraditional family system.

7.2.3 Group Membership

Human beings are born, and freely enter, into relationships with other human beings, even with human beings that do not share the same set of all common values, for example, the "duty club" that includes atheists and Christian members or even gay-straight alliances. Human beings acquire their identity through group memberships. Group membership suggests sameness; group exclusion suggests difference. Sameness and difference establish group boundaries, where members belong inside or outside the group. Within groups, there are role differentiations whose labeling and roles help to construct identity, for example, housewife, New Yorker, male, and religious.

Human beings are aware of their difference, yet difference does not eliminate the possibility of participating in relationships. By using "I," "we," and "they" language, difference suggests something plural and complex, even fragmented and problematic, about the universal group called humanity. Difference can lead to comparison and, at times, insecurity; for example, when I judge myself to be adequate or inadequate (cf. the effects of shame; note: no one can pass through life without ever experiencing shame). However, difference, once integrated through practical wisdom and scientific analysis, finds unity through an exchange of values and ideas.

Groups have expectations of individuals. Group expectations include requirements for membership and prescriptions for members, some of which differ according to label and role. Groups decide what is normal and what is abnormal. For instance, the historical effort within and without the Boy Scouts of America to accept and recognize homosexuals as full members (cf. despite the bad ruling in the US Supreme Court decision *Boy Scouts of America v. Dale*, 2000), as well as more recent social action in scouting to accept and recognize Trans Scouts. Thus, groups develop concepts of group identity and membership, which may or may not evolve or devolve through time—group members maintain senses of self and membership.

Though human beings are inclined toward social groups, they can also be critical of such groups by using their reflective capacity. Unlike animals whose actions are determined wholly by sense and appetite, human beings can choose principles of tolerance over and against principles of intolerance. A human being can step back intellectually and think about memberships that are inimical to human nature. For instance, a human being can step back, critically reflect on membership in groups like the Ku Klux Klan or the Oath Keepers, and decide not to join. One can also reject one's allegiance to a group that one is born into; for example, a citizen of the United States can emigrate.

7.2.4 Structural Violence: Guilt and Shame

Martin Luther King, Jr., wrote in *The Ethical Demands of Integration* that "Every man must be respected because God loves him. The worth of an individual does not lie in the measure of his intellect, his racial origin, or his social position. Human worth lies in relatedness to God."[20] At our disposal are the Hindu concepts of *Satyagraha* (nonviolent weapon) and noncooperation, whereas "no one need wait for anyone else in order to adopt a right course."²¹ In human history, structural violence has been endemic to group membership.

Structural violence is the systemic harm caused to human beings or human communities, which results from intolerance and discrimination, and systematic harm, where the intentionality or the purpose of the system is to cause harm.²² At the very least, structural violence leads to the marginalization (or ostracism) of individuals or groups who are viewed as different or as "others," not as the same as "us." Structural violence describes social structures—economic, political, legal, religious, and cultural—that stop individuals, groups, and societies from reaching their full potential.²³ In its general usage, the word "violence" often conveys a physical image; however, according to Johan Galtung, it is the "avoidable impairment of fundamental human needs or . . . the impairment of human life, which lowers the actual degree to which someone is able to meet their needs below that which would otherwise be possible."²⁴

Structural violence is often embedded in long-standing "ubiquitous social structures, normalized by stable institutions and regular experience" (cf. Galtung in Gilligan, 1997, p. 306). Once made an "other" or "othered," a person's flourishing is impaired. The possibility and potentiality for reaching one's fullest stable (integrated) identity as an individual and as a member of a group are also impinged on by structural violence (Young, 2011). In his chapter "Love, Law, and Civil Disobedience," Martin Luther King, Jr., noted:

> One seeks to defeat the unjust system, rather than individuals who are caught in that system. And that one goes on believing that somehow this is the important thing, to get rid of the evil system and not the individual who happens to be misguided, who happens to be misled, who was taught wrong. The thing to do is to get rid of the system and thereby create a moral balance within society.²⁵

A correlate effect of structural violence is the shame a victim feels (as distinct from the shame an agent wishes to produce, cf. the effects of picketing by the Westboro Baptist Church), where the agent inflicts violence and is the source of shame. Here, shame, as psychological violence, is an effect of structural violence. The shame a victim feels is different from guilt. Shame and guilt are both feelings; each has its own affective expression and bodily reaction, and each can be grounded in human conduct (to avoid guilt, I do what is morally right). Guilt is the feeling that results after a violation. Guilt arises from a sense that one has transgressed beyond the law or normative code of conduct. If I rob a bank, and in the process of robbing the bank hurt an employee and am soon caught by the police, I am certain to feel guilt. The shame a victim of structural violence or discrimination feels is a form of self-criticism or self-blame, which targets one's very being (identity) and not simply one's action. Such shame reduces feelings of joy and interest, causing human beings to feel at times humiliation and embarrassment. (In my Ethics section, I examine bad and good shame.) Martin Luther King, Jr., wrote in *Stride Towards Freedom*, "Whenever we are an object of criticism from white men, even though the criticisms are maliciously directed and mixed with half-truths, we must pick out the elements of truth and make them the basis of creative reconstruction."[26] We can remember what the great African American author James Baldwin wrote in his *Notes of a Native Son*: "I love America more than any other country in this world, and exactly for this reason, I insist on the right to criticize her perpetually."[27]

Still, the shame of a victim of structural violence typically expresses itself in the feelings of inadequacy: I am or am not a member of the group (ostracism) or I am offensive (disgusting) enough to someone or to a group to cause them a moral panic (or alarm). Another form of shame occurs through derogatory labeling. Recall for a moment what it might be like for an African American to be called an "N#$$er" or a homosexual to be called an "F#$%t." Such shame cuts away at our self-confidence and impinges on our ability to participate in loving relationships with others and actively engage the social life, for example, friendship and flourishing. (Note: This shame is different from the shame a rape or incest victim might feel, who at first might feel that he or she caused or is responsible for the act of violence.)

As far as these labels are based on beliefs about certain groups, we can raise questions about the validity of beliefs and subject these labels and beliefs to epistemological critique. I address these ideas with knowledge in my Epistemology section. Martin Luther King, Jr., reminded us that the whole structure of thought and knowledge seeking must change.[28] Further, for King, the real goal was "to awaken a sense of shame within the oppressor and challenge his false sense of superiority... The end is reconciliation; the end is redemption; the end is the creation of the Beloved Community."[29]

7.3 Epistemology

Epistemology is the study of knowledge and justified belief. Theories of knowledge answer questions about what we know as well as test the reliability of truth claims. Theories of knowledge typically integrate reason and sense experience. (Note: My term label equals the term *concept*; concepts are connected with beliefs.) As

James Cone, the African American theologian and father of Black Liberation Theology, noted, truth meant love for Martin Luther King, Jr., "the love of God and human love," neighborly, redeeming love, which generates the Beloved Community.[30] It is important to my framework for the Beloved Community to examine how we know things, but it is more important to my overall project on character formation and human flourishing. Elementary and secondary schools are the primary sites where most human beings study and acquire knowledge; attendance at college is not a given—hence, a recommendation for my readers to reflect on epistemological racism.

Knowledge can be practical, scientific, and interpersonal. In this section, I focus on these forms of knowledge as well as knowledge of socially constructed categories and the social world. (Other forms include spiritual and intuitive knowing.)

7.3.1 Three Forms of Knowledge: Knowing-How, Knowing-That, Knowing-You

The objects of knowledge are of various sorts and include: knowing how to do something; knowing objective facts about things, persons, and places; intimate personal knowledge of persons and interpersonal relationality; and knowledge of socially constructed categories. Each form is acquired somewhat differently. In this subsection, I treat the first three, reserving the fourth for later.

I know how to do things. For example, I know how to write. I know how to ski. This knowledge is usually acquired first by demonstration and with the help of another human being, and second by practicing what I learned to do. I can engage in a process of self-discovery and know more about myself.

I know objective facts about things, persons, places, nature, and so on. This knowledge normally takes a propositional form: I know that the Earth is a sphere; I know that I live in Queens; I know the United States of America is a nation, and many other facts. The general form of such knowledge can be expressed as "S (the subject) knows that P (the propositionally formulated fact)." More accurately, propositional knowledge is justified true belief. Thus, S knows that P only if S believes that P is true, and that S's belief that P is justified (by a reliable cognitive process). Thus, knowledge requires truth, belief, justification (warrant), and reliability. While truth, belief, and justification are (normally) necessary and sufficient for knowledge, I believe that reliability, the idea that one's justification rests on a reliable process, adds a cognitive check or a review to the mental process by which justified true belief becomes the knowing of objective facts. (Existential discovery is oblique.)

Normally, we acquire everyday propositional knowledge through these sources of knowledge: perception, introspection, self-discovery, memory, reasoning, and testimony. The African American poet, memoirist, writer, and civil rights activist Maya Angelou gifted us with a new understanding about the power of testimony! With perception, I know that a rose smells. With introspection, I can tell when I am tired. With self-discovery, I can tell that I am gay. With memory, I can remember my cell phone number. With reason, I explain how a car starts or why structural violence is wrong. With testimony, I can know the time and that my grandmother was Polish.

Scientific knowledge combines the sources we use in everyday knowledge in a systematic process of (evaluative, whereas the proper method equals good or bad science) inquiry. For instance, if I want to learn about the migratory habits of Australian Cockatiels (which I also have as pets), then I must study them in nature, examining trends in mating, nesting, and habitation. More precisely, I conduct observations (perceptions), record findings (memory), draw conclusions (reasoning), build on another's research (testimony), and so on. With science, I can also judge inferences (logic). Generally, scientific questions lead through a process of inquiry to answers that separate beliefs into categories of knowledge and opinion. The separation of beliefs into categories of knowledge and opinion requires critical self-awareness, which in science generally takes the form of qualitative or quantitative empirical tests.

Knowledge also comes from interpersonal relationships, for example, persons and interpersonal relationality. For instance, interpersonal relationships give us relational knowledge about how to express love appropriately or how to interact with people at work. Such relational knowledge starts in the family.

7.3.2 Knowledge of Socially Constructed Categories and the Social World

Our social interactions are heavily structured by beliefs about the attributes of people and the social meaning of those attributes. Although many of these have an ethical character (e.g., all children should be educated through the twelfth grade), some involve social definitions (e.g., a family is . . ., Americans are free people, etc . . .). Theologians like Gandhi and King asked questions about socially constructed categories, namely: Are such beliefs justified? Do such beliefs create or lead to justice and the dignity and worth of every human person?

For some human beings, knowledge of socially constructed categories is based on the beliefs they hear at home, during the process of child-rearing and through human development. For example, children learn from their parents about the positive effects of friendships, and that "friend" is identified as a social category. Children learn from their parents' opinions that it is good to have friends. For a negative example, recall that it was common during the pre-Civil Rights Movement for Southern White racist families to refer to African Americans as "N#$$ers" or "Coloreds." All of the many meanings associated with these vile terms shaped the way particular family members viewed, understood, mythicized, and knew African Americans. The beliefs these people had were justified in their view, on the basis of what they heard from people they trusted.

What we see from these two examples is that: (a) many social categories and labels are acquired via socialization; (b) many seem straightforward and innocent (friend, relative; girls, boys; baby, teenager; etc.) and fit everyday experience; but (c) some are derogatory, racist, and so on, and are rejected by people outside the group that maintains the labels. This difference between different categories—those we evaluate for acceptance and those we eventually reject—raises a critical question for epistemology. In the following section as well as my Ethics section, I elaborate on the key elements of an inquiry into the status of labels and beliefs in which they are based.

7.3.3 Critiquing Labels (Critical Social Inquiry)

All social categories are associated with perceptions of and beliefs about the group and its objective properties, for example, homosexuals are promiscuous. Such beliefs are not necessarily true beliefs: we can criticize them through objective inquiry. For example, we can subject the stereotypical belief "all homosexual men are promiscuous" to a process of inquiry grounded in scientific study; we can also collect counter-examples by actually socializing and having intimate relationships with people whom one is trying to understand. More broadly, negative labels and categories, beliefs, and common role-assumptions can be critiqued for validity in the following ways: (a) by locating testimonial injustice and bias, for example, because you are a N#$$er your testimony does not count, as in Harper Lee's 1960 novel *To Kill a Mockingbird*; (b) by checking the reliability of myths, opinions, and stereotypes against reason as well as empirical/scientific study (e.g., qualitative and quantitative scientific/social analysis); (c) by evaluating openness to dialogue (does the labeled party accept the label (e.g., believe wrongly and commit to the label, regardless of evidence)?; (d) by assessing the epistemic vice or virtue of the person advocating label/

belief, as in the speaker regarding intolerance vs. openness, epistemic vice: disposition to rash judgment and epistemic virtue: disposition to prudence (e.g., consider how one might assess the epistemic vice of former US president Donald J. Trump or his MAGA Movement); and (e) by investigating the limiting effects of negative labeling on human flourishing. In response to such critique, it is clear that as a free and critically reflective human being, I can accept or reject a negative label or category. Additionally, at times, mistaken beliefs that are central to our self-concepts may resist corrective experiences (such as women and motherhood) and not developing their creative social contributions and talents to their fullest capacity. For Gandhi, "No man can claim that he is absolutely in the right or that a particular thing is wrong because he thinks so, but it is wrong for him so long as that is his deliberate judgment."[31] This is the key to the success of soul-force,[32] to distinguish between doing right or doing wrong (harm).

I approach ethics having established an epistemology grounded in a process of inquiry. The task of my Ethics section is to present an ethics that provides criteria for evaluating and judging the moral appropriateness of social labels and the behaviors and institutions based on those labels.[33] This presentation is important because it helps in the response to the suffering, pain, and hurt caused by people who insult, bully (harass), stigmatize, or label other people as objects based on arbitrary characteristics (F@$$ot, N#$$er, K!<e, FA$$y).

7.4 Ethics

7.4.1 Introduction

Society has rules based on labels. Some discrimination and labeling are appropriate, as when we tell a legally labeled criminal sex offender that he or she cannot live near a school. How do we distinguish between the wrong and right labels and rules?

Notice four possibilities: (a) I can have an appropriate label and an appropriate rule, for example, male/female and roles regarding the use of one's gender-specific restroom; (b) I can have an appropriate label and inappropriate rule, for example, male/female and prohibitions against women in higher education; (c) I can have an inappropriate label and an inappropriate rule, for example, racist labels and Jim Crow laws targeting African Americans; and (d) I might have an inappropriate label linked with an appropriate rule.

For instance, society at large is not allowed to employ the label N#$$er when describing African Americans, but some rappers use the word N#$$er in their lyrics and/or African Americans can employ the term *N#$$er* colloquially within their communities as a term of brotherhood, as Tupac Shakur did in his 1993 rap album *Strictly 4 My N.I.G.G.A.Z.* and in the salutary phrase: "What up my N#$$er." (Note: The use and deployment of terms like N#$$er and Queer remain controversial.)

My method of evaluating or justifying labels and rules does not support moral arbitrariness or value neutrality, but rather the building of communities that respect differences and treat all group members benevolently. I take mutual recognition as the key idea. Mutual recognition, and the respect it entails, stresses the universal idea of our common humanity over and above more specific classifications. As rational agents, we expect to be treated as who we are by our nature, not like animals who are not autonomous and do not ask to be acknowledged for who they are.

More precisely, mutual recognition requires two kinds of respect: (a) we respect other people by recognizing them as ends in themselves, rather than things we value only for our exploitation; and (b) we respect people by recognizing their creative contribution to society. Only those social labels are morally appropriate which are consistent with these two kinds of mutual recognition. For instance, while a graduate student at Teachers College, Columbia University, I was a member of the graduate community of doctoral students, but, ultimately, I was a member of the human race. At Columbia University, I mutually recognized my peers as both workers in the field of education and as human beings whose desire is to flourish as they choose and to contribute creatively to society. Mutual recognition is crucial for personal identity formation and human flourishing. Human flourishing involves forming a stable (integrated) personal identity, social belonging, and constructive social contribution. One cannot stabilize one's identity if others do not affirm it or respect it as acceptable, and others must accept social contributions if they are to count as constructive contributions.

Mutual recognition is thus an essential component of human lives; the opposite of mutual recognition, disrespect, allows us to see why negative social labeling, insults, and insulting behaviors, as well as exclusionary institutions based on those labels, are wrong, for example, "N#$$er," racism, and the Ku Klux Klan. Negative labels are wrong because they deny a person something he or she needs to flourish, namely mutual recognition.

I now develop some implications of this ethical framework.

7.4.2 Avoiding Treating People as Mere Means or Children

During the US Civil Rights Movement, certain civil rights activists used the philosophical language of ends and means as a way to emphasize the sacredness of persons over things. In using the language of ends and means, civil rights activists told the world that human beings should be viewed as persons (ends) and not as things (means). These same civil rights activists understood the use of the label Negro by Southern White racists to generate a false category, which created a false reference to African Americans as mere means or, at best, as children who needed strong paternal correction. By identifying African Americans as mere means, Southern White racists refused to acknowledge African Americans as persons or ends in themselves, but reduced the quality of their "thingness," performance, and function; as such, they no longer considered them human. By treating African Americans as children, Southern White racists used paternalism to limit their capacity to flourish as autonomous agents and to problematize the African Americans' responsibility for their own flourishing. The effect of paternalism and objectification on the African American worked toward this end: economic and political gains for Southern White racists. The effect of paternalism and objectification on the African American also isolated African Americans, who had to bear their pain and affliction without a dignified place or access to the useful tools needed to communicate their suffering to the world. From the lessons of the Civil Rights Movement, we know that we cannot treat people as mere means or children; we must recognize all human beings as sacred, as ends in themselves. How?

Human beings recognize other people by respecting them as ends in themselves, rather than by reducing them to things or dependent human persons. That is, one respects the other's freedom or autonomy. These same people desire to live human lives and flourish freely (with dignity).

7.4.3 Disagreement Calls for Dialogue

Human flourishing requires freedom, and to respect someone as free is to respect that person as an end and an adult, not as a means or a child. When a person is reduced to his or her being as a means (e.g., a function, as having a determined-for-them life plan, and not recognized as a fully rational or relational being), their human flourishing is limited and their ability to be free diminished. As we recognize the "I" in the "thou," then our consciousness of "I" arises from the encounter of the "thou."[34] We are intrinsically tied to each other in love, hope, and solidarity; our critical reflection about being and belonging to each other is tied to our communion and community.

It follows from the idea of mutual recognition that laws should not frustrate human flourishing and should respect people's capacity for autonomy and conscience; consider the negative affect of the raft of so-called Trigger Laws in response to the US Supreme Court's recent overturning of *Roe v. Wade*. Human beings who are coerced by other individuals or groups act against their consciences; such coercion thwarts their capacity to flourish both as individuals and in interpersonal groups. But people sometimes disagree about what constitutes human flourishing and whether a given label/rule is appropriate or inappropriate.

The reality of disagreement grounds the need for dialogue: if we disagree (e.g., about the appropriateness of a rule against abortion), then mutual recognition requires that we enter into a dialogue—rather than just impose the will of a fraction of the population on some group or the majority of people in the United States. Openness to dialogue, attentive listening, and openness to experiencing the other are critical components of my ethical system, including the treatment of human beings as ends in themselves.[35] Integration of another person's thoughts into my thought system requires agreement, reciprocity, and adoption.

Dialogue is a good principle of moral inquiry: in dialogue, we treat others with both kinds of respect. We allow them to say what they experience and believe, and we acknowledge their valid contributions to the discussion. Thus, when we enter into an open dialogue with a willingness to experience the other openly, we let them speak for themselves as ends, not as projections of our own irrational fears and wishes, or desire to control another based on a religious conviction that is not universal or ubiquitous. Fears, wishes, and desires that are not rationally grounded limit human flourishing and negate positive social labels that are morally appropriate and consistent with the two kinds of mutual recognition already discussed earlier.

Usually, when two individuals or a group of people dialogue, they respect and recognize each other. With respect and recognition, dignity follows, and invalid ideas about individuals and groups are dismantled, for example, a woman who aborts her fetus, thus ending her pregnancy, is not a murderer. With dignity follows love of brother and sister, the shared desire to eliminate hatred, violence, and evil. When we are wrong about our ideas and conceptions about people, when we hear different perspectives about people, we can generate social norms that recognize men and women with dignity, mutual respect, and recognition. Thus, my ethics suggests that moral progress is, at times, birthed from the pursuit of mutual recognition and respect. As James Cone reminded us, Martin Luther King, Jr., proclaimed in a sermon at Dexter Baptist Church that "Through our sin, through our evil and through our wickedness, we have broken communities."[36] Perhaps, for King, the cross, where Jesus Christ hung, is the site of dialogue and reconciliation; it is, for him, the place from which Christ-in-this-world creates the Beloved Community between all races, peoples, and genders.[37]

Real dialogue leads to better solutions for social policy, assuming there is (a) a clear perception of the requirements for human flourishing in some area of law, and (b) the opportunity to synthesize point(s) of view, such that participants can change their positions or at least understand where the other side is coming from and provide the space for social differences. Through dialogue, injury and harm are avoided; with consensus, people are open to change and account for other people's position.

By bridging different viewpoints, a more complete and substantive conversation about community and the unity of human beings can evolve into a discourse about human flourishing. This approach aims to eliminate the effects of irrational individuals and isolated groups. Irrational individuals and isolated groups, who gather into tribes and factions according to beliefs and values, frustrate (to the point of preventing) the process of dialogue, as in the case of the Taliban. Furthermore, extremism, fundamentalism, factionalism, and tribalism prevent change, frustrate reciprocity, devalue interdependence, and enhance or intensify difference. Extremism, factionalism, and tribalism also lead to the isolation of tribal and factional members who appear more and more irrational and closed to dialogue; this is antithetical to many of the points covered in my Human Nature and Epistemology sections. To effect change, we must treat these individuals and groups with mutual recognition and respect. Clearly, this task is complex (nuanced), difficult, and slow, but from what we learned during the US Civil Rights Movement, it remains efficacious toward the end of eliminating the irrational anger and fear (and rigidity) felt by individuals and groups who are on the fringe.

7.4.4 Bad Shame and Good Shame: Acts and Ethics

Shame targets being. Since shame targets one's being, it is good only if the target is a corrupt character or behavior that one has become, such as a sexual predator or drunkard, among others. To conclude the Ethics section, I address two issues related to shaming. First, we need to develop some criteria for judging when shaming or something similar to shaming is morally appropriate, or, second, when the employment of shame is good (or constructive), as in feeling shame for what one has become, such as a drunk, or corrective as with a man's encounter with a brilliant female physicist. To be clear: if shaming can lead to enhanced flourishing, it is potentially good; if it shames someone for sowing prejudice, falsehood, and the like in a group, it can be good; if it shames someone by targeting a character or a behavior, it can be good; but if it excludes people arbitrarily and undermines or thwarts flourishing, it is bad.

For some, "good shame" leads to feelings of respect, of self-discovery, of antinarcissism, of the need to reassess (critically) one's culture, of awe (e.g., insight and the "aha" moment of self-discovery, e.g., how Ignatian Pedagogy and the *Ignatian Pedagogical Paradigm* can be used in public schools to develop and promote character formation of urban youth), of idealization, of reverence, or of protection from the effects of bad shame. Through good shame, men and women can critically reassess one's basic commitments and character. Ashamed of being a drunk, a person can take steps to get sober.

By contrast, the effects of bad or negative shame (induces) include feelings of helplessness, identity degradation (individual character discrepancy), disintegration, victimization, and anger. For some same-sex couples, the effects of negative shame are transmitted to members of their nontraditional family, and this limits their ability to flourish in a moral and ethical society that sees happiness, self-determination, and empowerment as more beneficial than discrimination, structural violence, and inequality. Thus, negative or bad shame is stigmatizing.

7.5 Philosophy of God and Religion

7.5.1 Introduction

Both Mohandas K. Gandhi and Martin Luther King, Jr., saw God as Truth. For Gandhi, human beings exist in a state of being (*Satya*), which is the right name of God.[38] For King, "God is able" in spite of the presence of evil.[39] I believe that Gandhi and King, like Ignatius of Loyola, desired that human beings become indifferent to the world insofar as the moral high ground and singleness in devotion to God generate the Gandhian concept of Swaraj and the Kingian concept of the Beloved Community, which Ignatius of Loyola grounded in his Spiritual Exercises in his First Principle and Foundation. Gandhi summarized such a pursuit of God-Truth, stating:

Therefore, the pursuit of Truth is true *bhakti*, devotion. Such *bhakti* is a bargain in which one risks one's very life. It is the path that leads to God. There is no place in it for cowardice, no place for defeat. It is the talisman by which death itself becomes the portal to eternal life.[40]

In this section, I am doing something different and new and related to God and to belief in God. First, I look at the Philosophy of God, toward the end of suggesting a way of reducing the effects of evil through forgiveness. Second, I look at the Philosophy of Religions, toward the end of integrating my Ethics section into a discussion about interreligious dialogue and interreligious interconnectivity. To do this, I found integrating philosophy and theology helpful. Herein rest some implications for how Ignatian Pedagogy and the *IPP* can be used in public schools without worry about evangelization, catechesis, or proselytization.

7.5.2 Philosophy of God: Reducing the Effects of Evil Through Forgiveness

In my Philosophy of God section, I deal with the challenges of evil to human flourishing, whereas Martin Luther King, Jr., still saw God as able.[41] Like King, rather than defend God's existence, I show how evil need not lead one to give up faith. More precisely, I show the compatibility of belief and evil at a practical level rather than a theoretical level—practical response: one that combines faith with recognition of evil. Belief provides additional demands (*sic* duties) on the response of believers to suffering and evil that do not hold for unbelievers. I thus do not "justify" faith with direct reasons for its truth—that is, I will not demonstrate the logical compatibility of evil and God's existence. Rather, I propose some considerations of the practical effects of faith for the believer's response to suffering and evil. With King, I agree that the American Romantic poet James Russell Lowell was right:

> Truth forever on the scaffold, Wrong forever on the throne,
> Yet that scaffold sways the future, and behind dim unknown,
> Standeth God within the shadow, keeping watch above his own.[42]

Our human experience includes two types of suffering: ontic and moral. Ontic suffering includes the suffering caused by natural forces such as an earthquake. Thus, ontic suffering does not assign moral responsibility.[43] Moral suffering results from evil, that is, culpable wrongdoing in a moral agent who acts as the source of the harm. For example, a member of the Ku Klux Klan who hangs a noose outside the home of an African American family is morally culpable for the harm caused to the African American family, their diminished well-being, and frustrated human flourishing. Yet, why did (and do) some Southern White racists still spit on or beat or cruelly treat African Americans even after (or as) they were integrated into society? How do people who believe in God respond to the suffering caused by human beings through evil actions?

Both believers and nonbelievers can respond by taking the moral higher ground, namely: (a) by working to eliminate evil that deprives men and women the capacity to flourish, and (b) by responding to the structural and social causes of evil with mutual recognition and respect. Believers have two additional requirements if their belief is to be practically compatible with the reality of evil: (c) taking evil as an opportunity for individuals and groups to call on God, to be merciful, and to forgive rather than to retaliate (cf. Gandhi's understanding of nonviolence); and (d) acknowledging the need for trust in God because evil is a mystery bound up with God's intentions (cf. King's understanding of God as able). With regards to the third requirement, practically, we can see in the Judeo-Christian tradition how to take evil *not* as grounds for rejecting God, but for *calling on God* for mercy and forgiveness (e.g., the Book of Job, the Psalms, Jesus's crucifixion) and trusting in God. (Note: I am open to the possibility that the third and fourth requirement may be adapted for use by nonbelievers, and pluralistically as the center (*sic* Truth) is de-centered or destabilized.) What about the place of forgiveness in this framework?

Again, forgiveness rests in the power of the victim. Forgiveness yields: (a) removal of hostility; (b) charity and compassion; (c) the possibility of apology and contrition; (d) re-integration of the evildoer into society; and (e) the promise of benevolent relationship based on mutual recognition, respect, and human flourishing. Goods of forgiveness for the victim and for the perpetrator include mutual recognition and respect; both increased mutual recognition and respect promise new beginnings at the time of new dialogues about sameness and difference between individuals and groups. Such is the power infused with love and justice that Martin Luther King, Jr., talked about in his text, *Where Do We Go From Here?* In it, he wrote:

> It will be power infused with love and justice, that will change dark yesterdays into bright tomorrows, and lift us from the fatigue of despair to the buoyancy of hope. A dark, desperate, confused and sin-sick world waits for this new kind of man and this new kind of power.[44]

7.5.3 Philosophy of Religion: Interreligious Dialogue and Interreligious Interconnectivity

The perpetual global War on Terrorism provides a helpful backdrop to my discussion about interreligious dialogue, whereas it is not an American problem but a globalizing and pluralistic world problem. (In city systems, some children will arrive at their public school with a beautiful array of religious values.) In the global War on Terrorism, a plurality of religions and religious institutions find themselves in conflict. By labeling all Muslims as "possible threats to national security" and all Christians as "the good guys," White supremacist society fits members of these two groups into artificial categories/labels and roles, for example, terror suspects and heralds of freedom. Negative labeling leads to more and more extremism, factionalism, fundamentalism, and tribalism; individuals and groups feel increasingly threatened by distorted claims about their identity. Negative stereotypes and depictions lead group members to the fringe, to being out-of-touch with reality (even anti-West), and toward an unwillingness to enter into interreligious dialogue or to accept interreligious interconnectivity. Thus, extremism, factionalism, fundamentalism, and tribalism threaten human flourishing by causing disunity.

As Gandhi and King knew, religion must and can be part of the solution, with its peculiar power to transform attitudes (peculiar: access to God and the power of God; exemplars include Pope Francis I and the Dalai Lama). To resolve the disunity caused by extremism, factionalism, fundamentalism, and tribalism, I employ the concept of interreligious interconnectivity. Interreligious interconnectivity takes as its core premise the mutual recognition and respect of group and nongroup members and the need for and promise of interreligious dialogue. As such, interreligious interconnectivity necessitates a critical, intersectional dialogue about the social world. Interreligious interconnectivity views the social world as good, that our view of humanity is enhanced by being open to interreligious dialogue and to experiencing the other who is not a member of one's religious institution but who also does not benefit from negative labeling, shame, structural violence, or discrimination.

The aim is to determine how different religious groups and nonbelievers can live together in a shared social world, characterized by mutual recognition and respect; certainly these men and women learned to co-exist as students in public schools. The aim is never to humiliate but to win over.[45] As James Cone noted in *The Cross and the Lynching Tree*, hate and humiliation "lead to violence and alienation, while love and the cross lead to nonviolence and reconciliation."[46]

Agape, the highest form of love and charity, is a realizable goal, according to Cone. Gandhi told us that "ruled by love, the world goes on."[47]

Commitment to interreligious interconnectivity and dialogue excludes negative labeling and religion-based exclusion of nongroup members from basic human recognition. Negative labeling frustrates a sense of belonging, which also fractures and fragments unity. Thus, the key is to get to specific issues in such dialogue, to reach pure soul-force. Interreligious interconnectivity and interreligious dialogue bring people to a discussion about God or gods, and our common humanity; for example, recognition of the latter enables members of different religions to recognize each other by their individual and species capacities, through labels, and as members of God's creation who share in the possibilities envisioned by Agape.

> In *An Experiment in Love*, Martin Luther King, Jr. defined Agape as meaning understanding, redeeming good will for all men. It is an overflowing love, which is purely spontaneous, unmotivated, groundless and creative. It is not set in motion by any quality or function of its object. It is the love of God operating in the human heart . . . It begins by loving others *for their sakes*.[48]

Agape is the orienting principle through which interreligious interconnectivity promotes human flourishing.

Interreligious interconnectivity promotes human flourishing in several ways: (a) by acknowledging that all men and women are children of God, thus ends in themselves; (b) by calling on different religions and different religious leaders not to politicize debate or treat members of other groups as mere means; (c) by emphasizing that a community of love and brotherhood cannot come into being without the fully moral behavior of all members; (d) by recognizing structural violence and discrimination for temporary success at best; and (e) by aiming toward a consensus that enhances interaction and cooperation between peoples and not negative judgment about an individual's or group's identity or worth. Interreligious interconnectivity and interreligious dialogue make it possible for mutual recognition and respect to help men and women to set aside self-interest and religious imperatives and to see that unity and solidarity are more important than extremism, factionalism, and tribalism.

For human beings to live together in one harmonious whole, they must reflect on interreligious interconnectivity. In looking to interreligious dialogue as a way to eliminate structural violence and discrimination, human beings must find guidance from their common human experience, for it is not enough to appeal ineffectually to good religious intentions. In sum, interreligious interconnectivity and interreligious dialogue are critical in promoting human flourishing.

7.6 Conclusion

Throughout this chapter, I demonstrated the influence of Mohandas K. Gandhi and Martin Luther King, Jr., on my understanding of how human beings flourish freely as individuals and as members of groups, and more specifically as members of the universal group called humanity. My conceptualization of human flourishing is consistent with reflections about my personal life and the lives of men and women who surround me in my work as a public school social worker. My conception of human flourishing welcomes pluralism and invites dialogue, for a Kairos is a moment open to all. As the comparative theologian John J. Thatamanil stated in a class lecture at Union Theological Seminary on April 14, 2015, "The Beloved Community is more than mere political or religious gesture, it is the end of the moral high ground, it begets change in the architecture of society, it addresses structural contradictions."[49] Thus, what is just changes.

When we consider our globalizing and interreligious world, we see the benefits of mutual recognition (mutuality), respect, and interreligious interconnectivity: We see a common core to human development and human flourishing. I believe that human flourishing helps direct us to the purpose of our life, each in our individual and unique way, as well as overlapping with other human beings. The common core constituent of my conception of interreligious interconnectivity and interreligious dialogue, which influences human development and human flourishing, is Agape.

Agape is the most durable love, the love that Martin Luther King, Jr., challenged society to adopt in his 1957 chapter "The Most Durable Power." It is the love of the Beloved Community, in both the eschatologically yet-to-come and the already here-and-present Kingdom of God.

More often than not, Agape, the moral high ground, has turned enemies into friends, has shaped history to reflect humanity's will to destroy structural violence, systemic harm, and social sin (*sic* all forms of evil). Agape should be our categorical imperative or duty (means) toward the end of goodwill for all people and groups; this same Agape brings about mutual recognition and respect. In many ways, our globalizing and interreligious world is facing modernity (again) head-first through a technological and environmental revolution. By also breaking down insularity, injustice, and groupthink, our globalizing and interreligious world acknowledges this reality: the effects of structural violence and discrimination, notwithstanding the test of time and space, are real. The effects of structural violence, discrimination, and shame can be reduced, even eliminated, by embracing goodwill for all people. King and Gandhi did not live in fear. Like them, we cannot be cowards. We must take risks, be honest, and have courage toward truth.

As Martin Luther King, Jr., told us, God is love. God is not an ideology! Love tells the truth; retaliation begets evil, evil multiplies evil.[50] King continued, "He who loves is a participant in the being of God. He who hates does not know God."[51] Agape (*sic* love) is the most durable power; it brings about the Gandhian concept of Swaraj and the Kingian concept of the Beloved Community, the Ignatian concept of *Magis*.

As we conclude our journey with Ignatius of Loyola, we can be mindful that it is God's will: that all God's creatures flourish as beings born in the image and likeness of God. Ignatius himself would agree that his pedagogical philosophy, as enhanced through the centuries of global student education and research, can be implemented in public schools without disrupting norms, for example, like the separation of church and state in the United States. Ignatius would then desire the fit between Ignatian Pedagogy, the Ignatian Pedagogical Paradigm (delivery of the curriculum/techniques of teaching), and public school programming in character formation (forming students to participate in the Beloved Community). Even with the clear separation of faith and education, Ignatius himself would agree that it is *All for the greater glory of God*. Ignatius himself would be grateful for that end and, in gratitude, exalt, pray, and encourage us to be like the Good Samaritan in the Gospel of Luke (Luke 10:25-37), to go and do likewise: to *Magis*.

Notes

Chapter 1

1 Benjamin Brenkert, *A Catechism of the Heart: A Jesuit Missioned to the Laity* (Searcy, AR: Resource Publications, 2020).
2 Pedro Arrupe, "Our Secondary Schools Today and Tomorrow," *Acta Romana Societatis Jesu* 10, no. 18 (1980): 257–76.
3 See website for New York City Department of Education at www.schools.nyc.gov.
4 See website for the International Baccalaureate Program at www.ibo.org.
5 Cristiano Casalini and Claude Pavur, SJ (Eds.), *The Way to Learn and the Way to Teach: Joseph de Jouvancy, S.J.* (Boston, MA: Institute of Jesuit Sources, 2019).
6 Current programming includes: Professor Lucy Calkins's Teachers College Reading and Writing Project Units of Study (www.unitsofstudy.com); social-emotional intelligence with the Aperture Education DESSA System Screener (www.apertureed.com); and afterschool character formation programs run by local Community-Based Organizations such as Woodside on the Move (www.woodsideonthemove.org) and Community Counseling and Mediation (www.ccmnyc.org).
7 My hope is for such a program of character formation to be developed in other public school districts and community schools. A future handbook will put forward the method for implementing this programming in public schools.
8 Gabriel Flynn and Paul D. Murray, *Ressourcement: A Movement for Renewal in Twentieth Century Theology* (Oxford: Oxford University Press, 2014).
9 In Chapters 4 and 5, specific school names are anonymized with the pseudonym Jesuit-Sponsored School (Chapter 4) and New York City Public School (Chapter 5). This anonymization further emphasizes the anonymity and confidentiality of my research as well as my analysis and demonstrates my respect and gratitude for all those about whom I write in order to focus on the content before the reader.
10 William Wordsworth, *The Collected Poems of William Wordsworth* (Digireads, 2018).
11 Ron Berger, *An Ethic of Excellence: Building a Culture of Craftsmanship with Students* (Portsmouth, NH: Heinemann, 2004), 154.
12 Richard Stanley Peters, *Ethics and Education* (New South Wales: George Allen and Unwin, 1986), 57.
13 President Joe R. Biden, Inaugural Address, January 20, 2021. President Biden was citing *City of God* by Augustine of Hippo (19.24). See Bill McCormick, SJ's essay

in America Magazine, *Joe Biden quote Augustine in His Inaugural Address: What Would the Saint Thin of Our Politics?* (January 20, 2021).
14 See Jesuit Constitutions, 1550 Formula, no. 1, v. 1–, pp. 2f., in Claude Pavur, *The Ratio Studiorum: The Official Plan for Jesuit Education* (Chestnut Hill: Institute for Jesuit Sources, 2005), 238.
15 Edmund P. Cueva, Shannon N. Byrne, and Frederick Benda, SJ (Eds.), *Jesuit Education and the Classics* (Newcastle upon Tyne: Cambridge Scholars Publishing, 2009), 13.
16 See O'Malley, as cited in in George W. Traub, *A Jesuit Education Reader* (Chicago. IL: Loyola Press, 2008), 43–5.
17 James Arthur, *The Formation of Character in Education: From Aristotle to the 21st Century* (New York: Routledge, 2020), 20.
18 Claude Pavur, *In the School of Ignatius: Studious Zeal and Devoted Learning* (Boston, MA: Institute of Jesuit Sources, 2019), 47.
19 Ibid., 47.
20 Ibid., 53.
21 See O'Malley, in Traub, 61.
22 Ralph E. Metts, SJ, *Ignatius Knew* (Washington, DC: Jesuit Secondary Education Association, 1995).
23 John Dewey, *Democracy and Education* (New York: The Modern Library, 1919), 99.
24 George E. Ganss, SJ, *Ignatius of Loyola: Selected Works and Spiritual Exercises* (Mahwah, NJ: Paulist Press, 1991), 278.
25 Documents of the Society of Jesus' General Congregation 35 (2008) were primary source.
26 Barton T. Geger, SJ, "What *Magis* Really Means and Why It Matters," *Jesuit Higher Education* 1, no. 2 (2012): 16–31.
27 Dewey (1919).
28 Geger, "What *Magis* Really Means," 279–80; also refer to the Jesuit Schools Network to see how they adapt Ignatius's educational ideals for their schools.
29 See Kane, in Traub, 370–8.
30 See Locke's *Some Thoughts Concerning Education* in Steven M. Cahn, *Philosophy of Education: Essential Texts* (New York: Routledge, 2009), 192.
31 Jocelyn Boryczka and Elizabeth Petrino, *Jesuit and Feminist Education: Intersections in Teaching and Learning for the Twenty-First Century* (New York: Fordham University Press, 2012).
32 Catharine MacKinnon, *Feminism Unmodified: Discourses on Life and Law* (Cambridge, MA: Harvard University Press, 1988); Judith Butler, *Gender Trouble: Feminism and the Subversion of Identity* (New York: Routledge, 2006).
33 See discussion of Rousseau's *Emile* and Kant's philosophy in Cahn (2009), 288.
34 Alan Sadovnik, Peter Cookson, Jr., and Susan Semel, *Exploring Education: An Introduction to the Foundations of Education* (Boston, MA: Allyn and Bacon, 2001),

132–5; see also Zaretta Hammond, *Culturally Responsive Teaching and the Brain* (Thousand Oaks, CA: Corwin, 2014) and Bryan Stevenson, *Just Mercy: A Story of Justice and Redemption* (London: Oneworld Publications, 2015).
35 Dr. Dean Brackley, in Traub, 109–10.
36 David Tyack and Larry Cuban, *Tinkering Toward Utopia: A Century of Public School Reform* (Cambridge, MA: Harvard University Press, 1995), 133.
37 Ibid., 84.
38 See Ernest Morrell, Rudy Duenas, Veronica Garcia-Garza, and Jorge Lopez, *Critical Media Pedagogy: Teaching for Achievement in City Schools* (New York: Teachers College Press, 2013), 16.
39 Ibid., 97–8.
40 Horace Mann and Mary Tyler Peabody Mann, *Life and Works of Horace Mann*, vol. 1 (RareBooksClub.com, 2012).
41 John Dewey, *School and Society* (New York: Cosimo Classics, 2008).
42 See David L. Fleming, SJ, *Draw Me Into Your Friendship: The Spiritual Exercises* (Boston, MA: The Institute of Jesuit Sources, 1996) and *Like the Lightning: The Dynamics of the Ignatian Exercises* (Boston, MA: The Institute of Jesuit Sources, 2004).
43 Harvey D. Egan, SJ, *Ignatius Loyola the Mystic* (Eugene, OR: Wipf and Stock, 2020).
44 John W. O'Malley, *The First Jesuits* (Cambridge, MA: Harvard University Press, 1993), 210.

Chapter 2

1 Charles Taylor, "Cognitive Psychology," in *Human Agency and Language (Philosophical Papers, Vol. 1)* (Cambridge, MA: Harvard University Press, 1985), 191.
2 John Dewey, *Experience and Education* (New York: Collier-MacMillan, 1969), 49.
3 Christopher Peterson and Martin E. P. Seligman, *Character Strengths and Virtues: A Handbook and Classification* (New York: Oxford University Press, 2004), 28–30.
4 Ralph E. Metts, *Ignatius Knew* (Washington, DC: Jesuit Secondary Education Association, 1995).
5 Dewey (1969), 18.
6 Cf. Erickson, in Peterson and Seligman, 60–2.
7 Ernest R. Hull, *The Formation of Character* (St. Louis: B. Herder, 1921), 168.
8 Cf. Encyclopedia.com.
9 Angela Duckworth, *Grit: The Power of Passion and Perseverance* (New York: Scribner, 2016).
10 Scott Seider, *Character Compass: How Powerful School Culture Can Point Students Toward Success* (Cambridge, MA: Harvard University Press, 2015).

11 Lawrence Kohlberg, *The Philosophy of Moral Development: Moral Stages and the Idea of Justice (Essays on Moral Development, Vol. 1)* (New York: Harper and Row, 1981).
12 Lisa Miller, *The Awakened Brain: The New Science of Spirituality and Our Quest for the Inspired Life* (New York: Random House, 2021).
13 See Howard Gardner, *Frames of Mind: Theories of Multiple Intelligences* (New York: Basic Books, 1985) and David Lazear, *Seven Pathways of Learning: Teaching Students and Parents About Multiple Intelligences* (Brookline, MA: Zephyr Press, 1994).
14 Duckworth, 65.
15 See Peterson and Seligman.
16 See Dewey (1969) and Metts.
17 Norma González, Luis C. Moll, and Cathy Amani, *Funds of Knowledge: Theorizing Practice in Household, Communities and Practice* (New York: Routledge, 2006).
18 Yvette Jackson, *The Pedagogy of Confidence: Inspiring High Intellectual Performance in Urban Schools* (New York: Teachers College Press, 2011), Chapter 5.
19 Martha C. Nussbaum, *Creating Capabilities: The Human Development Approach* (Cambridge, MA: Belknap Press, 2013). According to Jesus, as cited in the Gospels of Mark, Matthew, Luke, and John, life is not simply about pleasure since the human being acts in accordance with virtue (as well as conscience) to complete their life. For some, choosing virtue is better than not to choose, despite the fact that virtue in and of itself does not lead to the complete (whole) life or the self-sufficient life. In the arena of Human Capability, theorists like Amartya Sen (*Development as Freedom* [New York: Anchor Books, 2011], 200; Nussbaum, *Creating Capabilities*) asks: What are people actually able to do and to be? What real opportunities are available to them? How do people lead the life they see as valuable? Such questions are tied to beliefs about the fullness of human dignity and the worth of people. In such cases, the happiness or human flourishing of individuals is directly affected by poverty, domestic violence, and on and on. Sociologist Emile Durkheim noted that human beings cannot be happy unless their needs are related to their means (cf. Durkheim, *Selected Writings* [Cambridge: Cambridge University Press, 1972]). Martin Luther King, Jr., would go even further, seeing the human persons' (and primarily African Americans') flourishing as tied to their relationship as an end in itself, beings created in the image and likeness of God. King and other American Civil Rights activists notes the relationship between means and ends (James Melvin Washington (Ed.), *A Testament of Hope: The Essential Writings and Speeches of Martin Luther King, Jr.* [San Francisco, CA: Harper San Francisco, 1991]).
20 Cf. Paulo Freire, *Pedagogy of the Oppressed* (New York: Bloomsbury Academics, 1970), 85.

21 Linda Darling-Hammond and Jon Snyder, "Reframing Accountability: Creating Learner-centered Schools," in Anne Lieberman (Ed.), *The Changing Context of Teaching, Ninety-First Yearbook of the National Society for the Study of Education*, edited by Anne Lieberman, 11–36 (Chicago, IL: University of Chicago Press, 1992), 14.
22 Charles Abelman and Richard Elmore, *When Accountability Knocks, Will Anyone Answer?* (CPRE Research Reports, 1999), 140.
23 Metts.

Chapter 3

1 Cf. Timothy Walch, *Parish School: American Catholic Parochial Education from Colonial Times to the present* (Leesburg, VA: National Catholic Education Association [NCEA], 2016).
2 Cf. the Blaine Amendments, *Institute for Justice*, www.ij.org.
3 Cf. The Enabling Act of 1889, in Nick Sibilla, "The Court Case That Could Finally Take Down Antiquated Anti-Catholic Laws," *The Atlantic* (2020). www.theatlantic.com
4 Cf. Timothy Egan, "The Changing Face of Catholic Education," *The New York Times*, 2000. www.nytimes.com
5 Ibid.
6 Ibid.
7 Cf. Andy Smarick and Kelly Robson, "Catholic School Renaissance: A Wise Giver's Guide to Strengthening a National Asset," *Philosophy Roundtable* (2015). www.philosophyround table.org
8 Cf. Betsy Shirley, "The Era of the Parochial School Is Over: Meet the Catholic Educators Searching for What's Next," *America Magazine* (2019). www.americamagazine.org
9 Through the analytical lens of an emancipatory feminist theory of human flourishing (see Chapter 3), I appraise the contributions and efforts of these very different proto-feminist and feminist authors, who are Western, Christian, at times Post-Christian (cf. Daly) and White: (1) Radclyffe Hall, whose proto-feminist work (albeit autobiography) *The Well of Loneliness* became a classic of lesbian, religious fiction during the 1920s; (2) Mary Daly, whose radical treatment of feminist metaethics in *Gyn/Ecology* (1978) launched her onto the national stage and isolated her from men; (3) Elizabeth Johnson, who wrote the seminal text *She Who Is* (1992) about female and feminine images for God and established a criteria for a feminist hermeneutics; and (4) Jeannine Hill Fletcher, whose feminist voice acknowledges the work of her sisters and continues to push feminist boundaries in her latest work *Mother as*

Metaphor (2013). Moreover, it goes without saying that these texts, while analyzed chronologically (or side by side), are not equal, either in genre, audience, form, or content; each of them has a distinct thesis and purpose, if not contribution to proto-feminist and feminist movements. Each text is prophetic; that is, each text propels women's equality and women's rights movements, both then and now, toward actualizing an emancipatory feminist theory of human flourishing. I move on from these introductory remarks with great thanks to Elizabeth Cady Stanton, who during the "First Wave of Feminism" envisioned a theophany of women's rights and feminist flourishing (cf. Hill Fletcher, Kindle Location 4315). From Stanton onward, women have found different ways (cf. the Radicalesbians below) and involved different genres (cf. the rise and fall of the popular magazine *Ms.*) to make their voices heard. Whether in the early twentieth century, Victorian novels of Hall, or the twenty-first century theological anthropology and comparative theology of Hill Fletcher, women command greater visibility and greater mutual respect. Whether through the radical voice of Daly or the assimilating voice of Johnson, I ask these questions: Did these foresisters ever ask, What do the women they are writing to and about want from society, from men, or from their community, for example, in schools?

10 Carmen Luke and Jennifer Gore, *Feminisms and Critical Pedagogy* (New York: Routledge, 1992), 16–17.
11 Elisabeth Schussler-Fiorenza in her text *Wisdom Ways* (2001) coined the neologism kyriarchy (master rule), which locates the domination, subordination, and oppression of women in social structures and social systems.
12 Barry D. Adam, *The Rise of a Gay and Lesbian Movement* (Woodbridge, CT: Twayne, 1995), 42.
13 Please see Jeffrey Weeks's text *Against Nature: Chapters on History, Sexuality and Identity* (London: Rivers Oram Press, 1991), 4.
14 Thus, my appeal to understanding human flourishing starts with a discussion about Radclyffe Hall's appeal to human nature in general: this will bear greater fruit in my Hermeneutics section where I see Elizabeth Johnson discussing a methodology of interpretation that leads to mutual recognition and respect; it is Johnson who noted that the symbol functions to create meaning (cf. Elizabeth A. Johnson, *She Who Is: The Mystery of God in Feminist Theological Discourse* [Chestnut Ridge, NY: Crossroad, 1992], 4), while for Hall, the symbol functions to order desire. Nonetheless, it is Hall who through her classic lesbian text urged Victorian society to believe that all women share more than a biologically or socially constructed reality; they share a relational identity, one that Hill Fletcher spoke about through her comparative theological approach to interreligious dialogue.
15 Or more specifically, the tragic problem of sexual inversion (not sexual perversion) in a Post-First World War culture that ultimately put the novel on trial.
16 Mary Daly, *Gyn/Ecology: The Metaethics of Radical Feminism* (Boston, MA: Beacon Press, 1978), 99–101.

17 Ibid., 356.
18 Radclyffe Hall, *The Well of Loneliness* (Stellar Books, 1928/2013), 368–9). As such: Stephen Gordon is the image of Jesus Christ, who through her identity challenges cultural ideals of autonomy and self-sufficiency, as well as confronts the field of theology's involvement in the perpetuation of women's stigmatization by men.
19 In 1970, at the Congress to Unite Women the Radicalesbians wore t-shirts with the slogan "Lavender Menace" on them; they asked in their manifesto titled *The Woman-Identified Woman*: What is a lesbian? In their efforts to eliminate coercive identifications and gain autonomy, the Radicalesbians built the bedrock for radical feminism. In the spirit of Simone de Beauvoir, the Radicalesbians asked if one is born a lesbian, noting also that one becomes aware of their identity on a spectrum of lesbianism. The Radicalesbians wrote:

   What is a lesbian? A lesbian is the rage of all women condensed to the point of explosion. She is the woman who, often beginning at an extremely early age, acts in accordance with her inner compulsion to be a more complete and freer human being than her society—perhaps then, but certainly later—cares to allow her. (1)

   By stressing moral and prudential aspects of citizenship, the Radicalesbians manifesto set out to validate authentic lesbian selves, selves that are not viewed through the language of disability or disorder. Therefore, the Radicalesbians provide a historical context through which I view Mary Daly's radically feminist text on feminist metaethics, a text that has far-reaching implications for a philosophy of belonging and my conception of an emancipatory feminist theory of human flourishing.
20 Daly, 348.
21 Ibid., 37.
22 Ibid., xi–xii.
23 Daly, 2.
24 Ibid., 6.
25 Ibid., 18.
26 Scientific and linguistic knowledge combines the cultural-linguistic sources we use in everyday knowledge in a systematic process of inquiry. According to Daly (1978), if I want to learn about women's silencing by embedded fears, I can examine trends in grammar, women's capacity for self-integrity and efforts to silence women through curtailing reproductive rights (18–22). Better still is the connection between scientific inquiry and the original terms above: conduct observations (perceptions), record findings (memory), draw conclusions (reasoning), build on other's research (testimony), and so on. With science, I can also judge inferences (logic). Generally, scientific questions lead through a process of inquiry to answers that separate beliefs into categories of knowledge and opinion. The separation of beliefs into categories of knowledge and opinion requires critical self-awareness, which in science generally takes the form of qualitative or quantitative empirical tests.

27 Elizabeth A. Johnson, 43.
28 Ibid., 46.
29 Elizabeth A. Johnson, 171.
30 Hall, 324.
31 Elizabeth A. Johnson, 243.
32 Hill Fletcher (2013).
33 Ibid., Kindle Locations 2744–7.
34 Ibid., Kindle Locations 2725–8.
35 Contemplation of God is the highest end of metaphysics. As part of the ideal life, contemplation of God leads to our moral duty to respond both actively and reflectively to the needs of men and women who are affected by intolerable harms, including structural violence and discrimination.
36 Hill Fletcher, Kindle Locations 1271–3.
37 Hill Fletcher, Kindle Locations 877–81. For Hill Fletcher, negative labeling leads to more and more extremism, factionalism, and tribalism; individuals and groups feel increasingly threatened by distorted claims about their identity. Negative stereotypes and depictions lead group members to the fringe, to being out-of-touch with reality (even anti-West) and toward an unwillingness to enter into interreligious dialogue or to accept interreligious interconnectivity. Thus, extremism, factionalism, and tribalism threaten human flourishing by causing disunity.
38 As we have seen, through the integration of theology and philosophy, feminist approaches to human flourishing take as their primary concern the conversion of hearts and minds to generate the Beloved Community based on: self-knowledge, cooperation, an ethics of care, and discernment of future action. Self-knowledge, cooperation, and the discernment of future action can lead to greater calls for unity within the scope of the plurality of churches and religions. Without unity, religious communities devolve into sects and end in isolation.
39 For human beings to live together in one harmonious whole, they must reflect on interreligious interconnectivity. In looking to interreligious dialogue as a way to eliminate structural violence and discrimination, human beings must find guidance from their common human experience, for it is not enough to appeal ineffectually to good religious intentions. In sum, interreligious interconnectivity and interreligious dialogue are critical in promoting human flourishing.
40 Hill Fletcher, Kindle Locations 3086–9.
41 Hill Fletcher, Kindle Locations 3230–5.
42 When we consider our globalizing, interreligious, and postcolonial world, we see what Hall, Daly, Johnson, and Hill Fletcher described as the benefits of mutual recognition, respect, and interreligious interconnectivity: *we see a common core to human development and human flourishing, one that is perhaps grounded in a Feminist Ethics of Care.*

Chapter 4

1. This chapter discusses a Pilot Study.
2. (cf. www.nativitymiguel.org). (Please note, that at the time of the writing of this book more and more states like Maine and Arizona are allowing parents the use of vouchers to send their children to private schools, e.g., with taxpayer funds.)
3. The Jesuit-Sponsored School's *Student and Family Handbook 2008-2009*, 7–8.
4. Nancy L. Deutsch wrote in *Pride in the Projects* in 2008 that: "For racial and ethnic minority youth and young people living in poverty, it is not simply the categories of race or social class that influence their development but the everyday, personal experiences of discrimination that accompany these categories . . . And these experiences are determined not only by the relationship between people but also the relationships between people and social structures" (10).
5. Charles M. Blow, "No More Excuses?" *The New York Times* (January 23, 2009).
6. Gil G. Noam, Gina Biancarosa, and Nadine Dechausay, *Afterschool Education: Approaches to an Emerging Field* (Cambridge, MA: Harvard Education Press, 2003), 122.
7. David Von Drehle, "The Boys Are All Right," *Time Magazine* (August 6, 2007): 39–47.
8. Michael Gurian and Kathy Stevens, *The Minds of Boys: Saving Our Sons from Falling Behind in School and Life* (San Francisco, CA: Jossey-Boss, 2005); J. S. Kim and C. L. Streeter, "Increasing School Attendance: Effective Strategies and Interventions," in *The School Services Sourcebook: A Guide for School-based Professionals*, edited by Cynthia Franklin, Mary Beth Harris, and Paula Allen-Meares, 397–404 (New York: Oxford University Press, 2006); A. J. Sameroff and L. M. Gutman, "Contributions of Risk Research to the Design of Successful Interventions," in *Intervention with Children and Adolescents: An Interdisciplinary Perspective*, edited by Paula Allen-Meares and Mark W. Fraser (San Francisco, CA: Pearson Education, 2004).
9. Tommie Morton-Young, *After-school and Parent Education Programs for At-risk Youth and Their Families: A Guide to Organizing and Operating a Community-based Center for Basic Educational Skills Reinforcement, Homework Assistance, Cultural Enrichment, and a Parent Involvement Focus* (Springfield, IL: Charles C. Thomas, 1995).
10. George Yancy (Ed.), *What White Looks Like: African-American Philosophers on the Whiteness Question* (New York: Routledge, 2004).
11. G. C. Noam and J. Rosenbaum Tillinger, "After-school as Intermediary Space: Theory and Typology of Partnerships." *New Directions for Youth Development* (2004): 75–113.
12. Joseph L. Mahoney, Reed W. Larson, Jacquelynne S. Eccles, and Heather Lord. "Organized Activities as Developmental Contexts for Children and Adolescents," in

Organized Activities as Contexts of Development: Extracurricular Activities, Afterschool and Community Programs, edited by Joseph L. Mahoney, Reed W. Larson, and Jacquelynne S. Eccles, 3–22 (Mahwah, NJ: Lawrence Erlbaum, 2005).

13. Cf. Morton-Young.
14. Gil G. Noam and Nina Fiore, "Relationships Across Multiple Settings: An Overview." *New Directions for Youth Development* (2004): 9–16.
15. Gil G. Noam, B. M. Miller, and S. Barry, "Youth Development and Afterschool Time: Policy and Programming in Large Cities," *New Directions for Youth Development* (2002): 9–18.
16. Roger P. Weissberg, Karol L. Kumpfer, and Martin E. P. Seligman, "Prevention That Works for Children and Youth: An Introduction," *American Psychologist* (2003, June/July): 425–32.
17. Susan Goerlich Zief, Sherri Lauver, and Rebecca A. Maynard, *Impacts of Afterschool Programs on Student Outcomes: A Systematic Review for the Campbell Collaboration*. 2006. www.sfi.dk/graphics/ Campbell/reviews/afterschool_review.pdf (cf. SEDL Letter, 2008).
18. For the full report, please see www.sfi.dk/graphics/ Campbell/reviews/ afterschool_review.pdf.
19. Zief et al.
20. Cf. Etta Kralovec and John Buell, "End Homework Now," *Educational Leadership* (2001, April): 39–42; Beth M. Miller, "The Promise of After-school Programs," *Educational Leadership* (2001, April): 6–12.
21. Karl L. Alexander, Doris R. Entwisle, and Carrie S. Horsey. "From First Grade Forward: Early Foundations of High School Dropout," *Sociology of Education* 70, no. 2 (1997): 87–107.
22. 2008 Afterschool Year in Review, Afterschool Alliance, www.afterschoolalliance.org.
23. Cf. nccic.acf.hhs.gov/afterschool/mo.html#facts.
24. Cf. www.afterschoolalliance.org.
25. Cf. nccic.acf.hhs.gov/afterschool/mo.html.
26. Olatokunbo S. Fashola, *Building Effective Afterschool Programs* (Thousand Oaks, CA: Corwin, 2002); Noam et al. (2003); and Deutsch.
27. Cf. Kansas and Missouri Core Competencies for Youth Development Professionals in conjunction with Opportunities in a Professional Education Network (OPEN) Initiative in Missouri, the Missouri Afterschool Network (MASN), and the Kansas Enrichment Network (KEN) (2009).
28. Please see the full report at www.afterschool alliance.org/year_in_review.pdf.
29. Noam et al. (2003), 26.
30. Noam and Fiore.
31. See James S. Coleman, "Families and Schools," *Educational Researcher* 16, no. 6 (1987, August–September): 32–8; Deutsch; Noam et al. (2002).

32 Dan Kindlon and Michael Thompson, *Raising Cain: Protecting the Emotional Life of Boys* (New York: Ballantine Trade Paperback, 1999); N. Way and J. Y. Chu (Eds.), *Adolescent Boys: Exploring Diverse Cultures of Boyhood* (New York: New York University Press, 2004).
33 Fashola; Noam et al. (2003); and Deutsch.
34 Gurian and Stevens; Kindlon and Thompson; Christina Hoff Sommers, *The War Against Boys: How Misguided Feminism Is Harming Our Young Men* (New York: Simon & Schuster, 2000).
35 Noam et al. (2002); Noam and Tillinger; SEDL Letter (2008).
36 Susan L. Dauber, Karl L. Alexander, and Doris R. Entwisle. "Tracking and Transitions Through the Middle Grades: Channeling Educational Trajectories." *Sociology of Education* 69, no. 4 (1996, October): 290–307; Miller; and Noam and Fiore.
37 Zief et al.
38 Noam et al. (2002).
39 Ralph E. Metts, *Ignatius Knew* (Washington, DC: Jesuit Secondary Education Association, 1995), 28.
40 Please see Appendix A for a copy of the approved and administered survey.
41 Duane E. Monette, Thomas J. Sullivan, and Cornel R. DeJong, *Applied Social Research: A Tool for the Human Services* (Thomson Wadsworth, 2008).
42 Cf. *The Belmont Report*, http://www.hhs.gov/ohrp/humansubjects/guidance/belmont.htm.
43 Please see Appendix C.
44 See Appendix D.
45 See Appendix E.
46 See Appendix F.
47 See Appendix G.
48 Appendix G contains a table reporting the figures, including the mean difference.
49 For example, Saint Peter's Preparatory School, located in Jersey City, New Jersey (www.spprep.org).
50 Uri Bronfenbrenner, *The Ecology of Human Development: Experiments by Nature and Design* (Cambridge, MA: Harvard University Press, 1979).
51 The Jesuit-Sponsored School *Student and Family Handbook, 2008-2009*, 8.

Chapter 5

1 This chapter discusses a Pilot Study.
2 Peter-Hans Kolvenbach, *Go Forth and Teach: The Characteristics of Jesuit Education* (Washington, DC: Jesuit Secondary Education Association Foundations, 1986).

3 Ralph E. Metts, *Ignatius Knew* (Washington, DC: Jesuit Secondary Education Association, 1995), 37.
4 Ibid., 7–13.
5 See http://www.nysed.gov/special-education/blueprint-improved-results-students-disabilities.
6 Richard A. Villa and Jacqueline S. Thousand, *Leading an Inclusive School: Access and Success for All Students* (Alexandria, VA: ASCD, 2017).
7 Kathy Kolbe, *Pure Instinct: The M.O. of High Performance People and Teams* (Monumentus Press, 2004).

Chapter 6

1 Cf. Aristotle's *Nicomachean Ethics*, in which his concept of the good life, or *eudaimonia*, is grounded in a functionalist account of human nature. Karl Marx grounded happiness in the eradication of class and the formation of the State. Cf. Martha Nussbaum's *Creating Capabilities: The Human Development Approach* (Cambridge, MA: Belknap Press, 2013). For the psychiatrist Carl Jung (1966), the archetypal Self is the Christ, specifically in his Chapter "Christ, A Symbol of the Self" in Psychology and Religion. Neil Messer placed the conversation about the theology of human flourishing in disability studies in his text *Flourishing: Health, Disease, and Bioethics in Theological Perspective* (Grand Rapids, MI: William Eerdmans, 2013).
2 See Richard Dawkins, *The God Delusion* (Boston, MA: Mariner Books, 2008) and Christopher Hitchens, *God Is Not Great: How Religion Poisons Everything* (New York: Twelve, 2009).
3 David Tyack and W. Tobin, "The 'Grammar' of Schooling: Why Has It Been So Hard to Change?" *American Education Research Journal* 31, no. 3 (1994): 453–79.
4 Norma González, Luis C. Moll, and Cathy Amani, *Funds of Knowledge: Theorizing Practice in Household, Communities and Practice* (New York: Routledge, 2006).
5 Through his *Spiritual Exercises*, Ignatius defined and expanded his concept of *Suscipe*, the receiving and taking up of Christ to actualize the *telos* (sic end) of human freedom and human flourishing (cf. Karl Rahner's [1967] *Spiritual Exercises* and John Kane's *Building the Human City: William F. Lynch's Ignatian Spirituality for Public Life*). Such an experience of human flourishing tied to Ignatian Spirituality has great import for creating and implementing programs of character formation in the NYC DOE.
6 Denise Yarbough wrote that "embodied persons live in relationship. Relationship is dialogical, it requires listening and speaking, loving and embracing, and with genuine relationship comes the risk of personal transformation in the context of

increasing intimacy with the other" (in Zachary Guiliano and Charles M. Stang (Eds.)). *The Open Body: Chapters in Anglican Ecclesiology* (Pieterlen, Switzerland: Peter Lang, 2012). Also, please Aristotle's *Nicomachean Ethics*, specifically Book 10, Chapters 6–8.

7   Aristotle examined the good for individuals and community members in his text *Nicomachean Ethics*. He selected happiness (*eudaimonia*) because he believed human beings (rational agents) deliberate and choose thoughts and actions that can lead to their ultimate good (*sic telos* or end). Aristotle understood that human beings seek happiness for its own sake, and other things for the sake of happiness (its features being morality and virtue). To be an ultimate end, happiness is to be complete (or whole—*telos*). Other interpretations of human flourishing include: the perfectionist, the biological, the rational-end, and human welfare (cf. Charles Taylor, *Sources of the Self: The Making of Modern Identity* [1992] and Neil Messer, *Flourishing* [2013]). These interpretations each look at human nature through the lens of perfectibility, health and prosperity, human choice, and virtuous activity. For Aristotle, practical reason guides human beings (as rational agents) toward the good. The human good for him is located in the soul. My research challenges the ideology that the human end goal, for example, possessions, cannot simply be for life, or life more abundant, for they fail to address the fact that humans in situ "do not live by bread alone" (cf. DT 8 and MT/LK 4).

8   Ignatius's letter to the Members of the Society in Portugal, dated March 26, 1553, from *Ignatius of Loyola: Letters and Instructions* (2006).

9   See John English's *Spiritual Freedom: From an Experience of the Ignatian Exercises to the Art of Spiritual Guidance* (Chicago, IL: Loyola Press, 1995).

10 Cf. Selim Algar, Susan Edelman, and Conor Skelding's article in *The New York Post* (2021) and Alex Zimmerman's article in *Chalkbeat New York* (2021).

11 Paulo Gamberini, "Ignatian Spirituality and Anglican Ethos: A Family Resemblance," *One in Christ* 49 (2015): 2–21 and "Anglicanism and Ignatian Spirituality," in Robert J. Daly and T. Hughes (Eds.), *Ecumenism and Ignatian Spirituality: Proceedings of the 22nd International Congress of Jesuit Ecumenists* (Institute for Advanced Jesuit Studies, Boston College, 2016), 119–44. I wrote about the relationship between Ignatian Spirituality and Episcopalianism in a blog post for the Episcopal Café; see Benjamin Brenkert, "The Magazine: Lost and Found Through the BCP," 2015, https://www.episcopalcafe.com/the-magazine-lost-and-found-through-the-bcp; Joyce Hugget, "Why Ignatian Spirituality Hooks Protestants," *The Way* 68 (1990): 22–34.

12 See John W. O'Malley, *The Jesuits: Cultures, Sciences and the Arts, 1540-1773* (2015) and Ronald Modras, *Ignatian Humanism: A Dynamic Spirituality for the Twenty-First Century* (Chicago, IL: Loyola Press, 2004). Ignatius of Loyola used the Spanish *tu amor* to refer to love for God. Ignatius sought to help prayers toward a love-response to God, one that grounds human flourishing in a God-directed "give me

love of you." See Michael Ivens's *Understanding the Spiritual /Exercises: A Handbook for Retreat Directors* (Herefordshire: Gracewing Publishing, 2000). Cf. Ignatius's *Autobiography*; Ribadeneira's *Life of Ignatius*; George Ganss's *The Jesuits: Their Spiritual Doctrine and Practice: A Historical Study* (1964); Juan Luis Segundo's *The Christ of the Ignatian Exercises* (1987); and David L. Fleming's *Like the Lightning: The Dynamics of the Ignatian Exercises* (Boston, MA: Institute of Jesuit Sources, 2004).

13 Claude Pavur, *In the School of Ignatius: Studious Zeal and Devoted Learning* (Boston, MA: Institute of Jesuit Sources, 2019), 13.

Chapter 7

1 Abraham Joshua Heschel, *The Prophets: An Introduction, Vol. I* (New York: Harper Torchbooks, 1962), 138.
2 Cf. Psalms 23:1 and 73:26.
3 Other interpretations of human flourishing include: the perfectionist, the biological, the rational-end, and human welfare. These interpretations each look at human nature as perfectible; vulnerability and affliction, health and prosperity; human choice; and virtuous activity.
4 Robert Merton (1968) commented about the self-fulfilling prophecy that "refers to a process in which the false definition of a situation produces behavior that, in turn, makes real the originally falsely defined situation" (in M. N. Marger (Ed.), *Race and Ethnic Relations: American and Global Perspective* (10th ed.) (Boston, MA: Cengage Learning, 2015), 15). Often, the dominant *race* has the ability to label the minority race negatively, for example, inferior; the negative effects of this are discussed in my sections on structural violence, negative labeling, and shame.
5 Marger, 18.
6 Flavio Marsiglia and Stephen Kulis, "The Intersectionality of Race and Ethnicity with Other Factors," in *Diversity, Oppression, and Change* (2nd ed.), 52–72 (Houston, TX: Lyceum Books, 2015b), 12–13.
7 Marger, 28–30.
8 A key idea associated with moral flourishing and human flourishing is social interaction, especially regarding different social milieus and historical contexts, for example, settled moral matters where slavery is wrong vs. abortion.
9 Mohandas K. Gandhi, *Mahatma Gandhi: The Essential Writings* (New York: Oxford University Press, 2008), 90.
10 Ibid., 258.
11 Ibid., 90.
12 Marsiglia and Kulis, 52–70.

13 Benjamin Brenkert, *A Catechism of the Heart: A Jesuit Missioned to the Laity* (Searcy, AR: Resource Publications, 2020).
14 Flourishing involves the development of species capacities (e.g., intellect), but the particular form this development takes depends on the individual. Flourishing realizes not just any possibility, but natural species capacities, for example, for nourishment, shelter, social relationships, and the like.
15 Merton et al. in 1957 defined "socialization" as "the process by which people selectively acquire the values and attitudes, the interests, skills, and knowledge—in short, the culture—current in the groups of which they are, or seek to become, members . . . Socialization takes place primarily through social interaction with people who are significant for the individual" (287). Merton et al. suggested in *Some Preliminaries to a Sociology of Medical Education* that socialization leads to induction into culture; socialization occurs throughout the life cycle (40–1). Merton et al. defined "to socialize" as "to render social, to shape individuals into members of groups (whatever they may be—familial, religious or professional)"; this definition is descriptive (289).
16 Jennifer Roback Morse, in "No Families, No Freedom: Human Flourishing in a Free Society," wrote that "The family teaches the ability to trust, cooperate, and self-restrain . . . the family teaches the skills of individual self-governance," in Ellen Frankel Paul, Fred D. Miller, Jr., and Jeffrey Paul [Eds.], *Human Flourishing* (Cambridge University Press, 1999), 290. Morse added that as infants we are helpless, needy, and immature, and that in the process of growing up, human beings learn there is more to life than the satisfaction of bodily appetites (294–5).
17 D. J. Garrow, *Bearing the Cross: Martin Luther King, Jr., and the Southern Christian Leadership Conference* (New York: Perennial Classics, 1999), 33.
18 Esther Urdang, *Human Behavior in the Social Environment: Interweaving the Inner and Outer Worlds* (The Haworth Social Work Practice Press, 2015), 205.
19 See Urdang.
20 James Melvin Washington (Ed.), *A Testament of Hope: The Essential Writings and Speeches of Martin Luther King, Jr.* (San Francisco, CA: Harper San Francisco, 1991), 122.
21 Gandhi, 94.
22 Structural violence can be broken down into two parts, one that suggests a policy component (structural) and one that suggests a judgment (violence). When speaking about structural violence, we must always be open to hearing and learning from another side, especially by implementing dialogue. "Because they seem so ordinary in our ways of understanding the world, they appear almost invisible. Disparate access to resources, political power, education, health care, and legal standing are just a few examples. The [concept] of structural violence is linked very closely to social injustice and the social machinery of oppression" (Paul E. Farmer, B. Nizeye, S. Stulac, and S. Keshavjee, "Structural Violence and Clinical Medicine,"

PLOS Medicine 3, no. 10 (2006, October): 1686–91.). Systems of structural violence and discrimination that cause, for example, homosexuals shame also perpetuate the universal homosexual victim. Such a reality (e.g., for homosexuals) is inconsistent with my definition of human flourishing.

23 Gandhi on the Transforming societies (2008), 67–132.
24 Johan Galtung, *Kultuerlle gewalt*. Der Burger im Staat 43 (1993): 106; cf. Farmer et al..
25 Washington, 47.
26 Washington, 489.
27 James Baldwin, *Notes of a Native Son* (Boston, MA: Beacon Press, 1955).
28 See *Where Do We Go From Here?* in Washington, 250–2.
29 Garrow, 81.
30 James H. Cone, *The Cross and the Lynching Tree* (Maryknoll, NY: Orbis Books, 2011), 126.
31 Gandhi, 319.
32 Ibid.
33 There are different approaches and focuses to ethics: the good life, conduct, virtue, among others. Ethics is normative, as such ethics should be differentiated from science.
34 Martin Buber, *I and Thou* (New York: Touchstone Press, 1971).
35 Douglas B. Rasmussen, in Ellen Frankel Paul, Fred D. Miller, Jr., and Jeffrey Paul (Eds.), *Human Flourishing* (Cambridge University Press, 1999) wrote:
It remains the case that in order to flourish people must be capable of transcending their own perspectives or points of view.... It is certainly true that the achievement of human flourishing requires individuals at times to adopt perspectives different from their own. Taking a perspective other than one's own—whether it is ideal, that of a friend, or that of any human being—is a valuable instrument for practical wisdom on agent-relative view of human flourishing. An individual's moral growth, in both its personal and interpersonal dimensions, requires that this procedure be used, because flourishing requires learning about one's potentialities and understanding others. (25)
36 Cone, 127.
37 Ibid.
38 Gandhi, 44–6.
39 Washington, 504–9.
40 Gandhi, 46.
41 Washington, 504–9.
42 Washington, 507.
43 Moral evil can also produce ontic evils and vice versa, as when someone is denied medical care and, as a result, suffers from an untreated malady. Ultimately, we must

conclude that an earthquake is not an evil in itself, although human beings can be held responsible for how they respond to the victims. Intolerable harm caused by moral evil is preventable.

44 Washington, 597.
45 King, *The Power of Nonviolence,* in Washington, 13.
46 Cone, 71.
47 Gandhi, 316.
48 Washington, 19.
49 John J. Thatamanil and Cornel West, Class Lecture Notes from Gandhi and King, Union Theological Seminary, New York, April 14, 2015.
50 Garrow, 68.
51 Washington, 11.

Bibliography

Abelman, Charles, and Richard Elmore. *When Accountability Knocks, Will Anyone Answer?* CPRE Research Reports, 1999.

Adam, Barry D. *The Rise of a Gay and Lesbian Movement.* Woodbridge, CT: Twayne, 1995.

Afterschool Alliance. *Afterschool Alliance Backgrounder: Formal Evaluations of Afterschool Programs.* Afterschool Alliance, 2003. www.afterschoolalliance.org/issuebr.cfm

Alexander, Karl L., Doris R. Entwisle, and Carrie S. Horsey. "From First Grade Forward: Early Foundations of High School Dropout." *Sociology of Education* 70, no. 2 (1997): 87–107.

Alison, James. *On Being Liked.* Chestnut Ridge, NY: Crossroad, 2003.

Allen-Meares, Paula, and Mark W. Frase. *Intervention with Children and Adolescents: An Interdisciplinary Perspective.* San Francisco, CA: Pearson Education, 2004.

Allyn, Pam, and Ernest Morrell. *Every Child a Super Reader: 7 Strengths for a Lifetime of Independence, Purpose and Joy.* New York: Scholastic, 2022.

Aristotle, and D. Chase. *Nicomachean Ethics.* SDE Classics, 2019.

Arrupe, Pedro. "Our Secondary Schools Today and Tomorrow." *Acta Romana Societatis Jesu* 10, no. 18 (1980): 257–76.

Arthur, James. *The Formation of Character in Education: From Aristotle to the 21st Century.* New York: Routledge, 2020.

Augustine of Hippo. *City of God*, ed. H. Bettenson. New York: Penguin Classics, 2004.

Baldwin, James. *Notes of a Native Son.* Boston, MA: Beacon Press, 1955.

Baldwin, James. *Collected Essays*, ed. Toni Morrison. New York: The Library of America, 1998.

Baldwin, James. *Early Novels and Stories*, ed. Toni Morrison. New York: The Library of America, 1998.

Berg, Robert C., and Garry L. Landreth. *Group Counseling: Concepts and Procedures* (2nd ed.). Accelerated Development, Muncie, IN: Taylor and Francis, 1990.

Berger, Ron. *An Ethic of Excellence: Building a Culture of Craftsmanship with Students.* Portsmouth, NH: Heinemann, 2004.

Bleasdale, Jane E., and Julie A. Sullivan. *Social Conscience and Responsibility: Teaching the Common Good in Secondary Education.* Washington, DC: Rowman and Littlefield, 2020.

Bloomfield, David C. *American Public Education Law.* Pieterlen, Switzerland: Peter Lang Primer, 2016.

Blow, Charles M. "No More Excuses?" *The New York Times*, January 23, 2009.

Bonk, Curtis J., and Meina Zhu (Eds.). *Transformative Teaching Around the World: Stories of Cultural Impact, Technology Integration and Innovative Pedagogy*. New York: Routledge, 2022.

Booth, Wayne C., and Kate L. Turabian. *A Manual for Writers of Research Papers, Theses, and Dissertations*. Chicago, IL: The University of Chicago Press, 2013.

Boryczka, Jocelyn M., and Elizabeth A. Petrino. *Jesuit and Feminist Education: Intersections in Teaching and Learning for the Twenty-First Century*. New York: Fordham University Press, 2012.

Brenkert, Benjamin. *The Magazine: Lost and Found Through the BCP*. 2015. https://www.episcopal café.com/the-magazine-lost-and-found-through-the-bcp

Brenkert, Benjamin. *A Catechism of the Heart: A Jesuit Missioned to the Laity*. Searcy, AR: Resource Publication, 2020.

Bricker-Jenkins, Mary, Nancy R. Hooyman, and Naomi Gottlieb (Eds.). *Feminist Social Work Practice in Clinical Settings*. Thousand Oaks, CA: Sage, 1991.

Bronfenbrenner, Uri. *The Ecology of Human Development: Experiments by Nature and Design*. Cambridge, MA: Harvard University Press, 1979.

Brown, K. "The Power of Perception: Skin Tone Bias and Psychological Well-being for Black Americans." In *Racial Identity in Context: The Legacy of Kenneth B. Clark*, edited by G. Philogéne, 111–23. Washington, DC: American Psychological Association, 2003.

Buber, Martin. *I and Thou*. New York: Touchstone Press, 1971.

Butler, Judith. *Gender Trouble: Feminism and the Subversion of Identity*. New York: Routledge, 2006.

Cahn, Steven M. *Philosophy of Education: Essential Texts*. New York: Routledge, 2009.

Canda, Edward R., and Leola Dyrud Furman. *Spiritual Diversity in Social Work Practice: The Heart of Helping*. New York: The Free Press, 1999.

Card, Claudia. *The Atrocity Paradigm: A Theory of Evil*. New York: Oxford University Press, 2002.

Carroll, Julie, and Meredith Minkler. "Freire's Message for Social Workers: Looking Back, Looking Ahead." *Journal of Community Practice* 8, no. 1 (2000): 21–30.

Carter, Samuel Casey. *On Purpose: How Great School Cultures Form Strong Character*. Thousand Oaks, CA: Corwin, 2011.

Carver, Raymond, William L. Stull, and Maureen P. Carroll (Eds.). *Collected Essays*. New York: The Library of America, 2009.

Casalini, Cristiano, and Claude Pavur, SJ (Eds.). *Jesuit Pedagogy 1540–1616: A Reader*. Boston, MA: Institute of Jesuit Sources, 2016.

Casalini, Cristiano, and Claude Pavur, SJ (Eds.). *The Way to Learn and the Way to Teach: Joseph de Jouvancy, S.J.* Boston, MA: Institute of Jesuit Sources, 2019.

Charmaz, Kathy. "The Grounded Theory: An Explication and Interpretation." In *Contemporary Field Research: A Collection of Readings*, edited by R. Emerson. New York: Little Brown, 1988.

Coatsworth, J. Douglas, and David E. Conroy. "Youth Sport as a Component of Organized Afterschool Programs." *New Directions for Youth Development* 2007, no. 115 (2007): 57–74.

Coffman, Julia. *Learning from Logic Models: An Example of a Family/School Partnership Program*. Cambridge, MA: Harvard Family Research Project, 1999.

Coleman, James S. "Families and Schools." *Educational Researcher* 16, no. 6 (1987, August–September): 32–8.

Cone, James H. *The Cross and the Lynching Tree*. Maryknoll, NY: Orbis Books, 2011.

Cone, James H. *Martin and Malcolm and America: A Dream or a Nightmare*. Maryknoll, NY: Orbis Books, 2012.

Cooper, Marsha G., and Joan Granucci Lesser. *Clinical Social Work Practice: An Integrated Approach*. Boston, MA: Allyn and Bacon, 2002.

Cueva, Edmund P., Shannon N. Byrne, and Frederick Benda (Eds.). *Jesuit Education and the Classics*. Cambridge Scholars Publishing, 2009.

Daly, Mary. *Gyn/Ecology: The Metaethics of Radical Feminism*. Boston, MA: Beacon Press, 1978.

Darling-Hammond, Linda, and Jon Snyder. "Reframing Accountability: Creating Learner-centered Schools." In *The Changing Context of Teaching, Ninety-First Yearbook of the National Society for the Study of Education*, edited by Anne Lieberman, 11–36. Chicago, IL: University of Chicago Press, 1992.

Dauber, Susan L., Karl L. Alexander, and Doris R. Entwisle. "Tracking and Transitions Through the Middle Grades: Channeling Educational Trajectories." *Sociology of Education* 69, no. 4 (1996, October): 290–307.

Davies, Don, Anne T. Henderson, Vivian R. Johnson, and Karen L. Mapp. *Beyond the Bake Sale: The Essential Guide to Family-School Partnerships*. New York: The New Press, 2007.

Dawkins, Richard. *The God Delusion*. Boston, MA: Mariner Books, 2008.

DeRoch, Edward F., and Mary M. Williams. *Educating Hearts and Minds: A Comprehensive Character Education Framework*. Thousand Oaks, CA: Corwin, 2001.

Deutsch, Nancy L. *Pride in the Projects: Teens Building Identities in Urban Contexts*. New York: New York University Press, 2008.

Dewey, John. *Democracy and Education*. New York: The Modern Library, 1919.

Dewey, John. *Human Nature and Conduct: An Introduction to Social Psychology*. New York: The Modern Library 1922.

Dewey, John. *Experience and Education*. New York: Collier-MacMillan, 1969.

Dewey, John. *School and Society*. New York: Cosimo Classics, 2008.

Dister, John E. *A New Introduction to the Spiritual Exercises of St. Ignatius*. Collegeville, MN: The Liturgical Press, 1993.

Drago-Severson, Ellie. *Helping Educators Grow: Strategies and Practices for Leadership Development*. Cambridge, MA: Harvard Education Press, 2015.

Duckworth, Angela. *Grit: The Power of Passion and Perseverance.* New York: Scribner, 2016.

Duminuco, SJ, Vincent J. (Ed.). *The Jesuit Ratio Studiorum: 400th Anniversary Perspectives.* New York: Fordham University Press, 2000.

Durkheim, Émile. *Selected Writings.* Cambridge, MA: Cambridge University Press, 1972.

Eccles, Jacquelynne S. "The Development of Children Ages 6 to 14." *The Future of Children: When School Is Out* 9, no. 2 (1999, Fall): 30–44.

Egan, SJ, Harvey D. *Ignatius Loyola the Mystic.* Eugene, OR: Wipf and Stock, 2020.

Egan, Timothy. "The Changing Face of Catholic Education." *The New York Times*, 2000. www.nytimes.com

Elmore, Richard F. "Change and Improvement in Education." In *A Nation Reformed?*, edited by D. Gordon. Cambridge, MA: Harvard Education Press, 2003.

Emdin, Christopher. *Urban Science Education for the Hip-Hop /Generation: Essential Tools for the Urban Science Educator and Researcher.* Rotterdam, Holland: Sense Publishers, 2010.

Emdin, Christopher. *For White Folks Who Teach in the Hood...and the Rest of Ya'll Too: Reality Pedagogy and Urban Education.* Boston, MA: Beacon Press, 2016.

Emdin, Christopher. *Ratchetdemic: Reimagining Academic Success.* Boston, MA: Beacon Press, 2021.

Emdin, Christopher. *Steam, Steam, Make, Dream: Reimagining the Culture of Science, Technology, Engineering and Mathematics.* Rexford, NY: International Center for Leadership in Education, Inc., 2022.

English, John. *Spiritual Freedom: From an Experience of the Ignatian Exercises to the Art of Spiritual Guidance.* Chicago, IL: Loyola Press, 1995.

Epstein, Joyce L., and Karen Clark Salinas. "Partnering with Families and Communities." *Educational Leadership* 61, no. 8 (2004): 12–18.

Erickson, Ansley T., and Ernest Morrell. *Educating Harlem: A Century of Schooling and Resistance in the Black Community.* New York: Columbia University Press, 2019.

Evans, Robert. "Reach and Realism, Experience and Hope." In *The Human Side of School Change*, 289–99. San Francisco, CA: Jossey-Bass, 1996.

Farina, Carmen, and Laura Kotch. *School Leader's Guide to Excellence: Collaborating Our Way to Better Schools.* Portsmouth, NH: Heinemann, 2014.

Farmer, Paul E., Bruce Nizeye, Sara Stulac, and Salma Keshavjee. "Structural Violence and Clinical Medicine." *PLOS Medicine* 3, no. 10 (2006, October): 1686–91.

Fashola, Olatokunbo S. *Building Effective Afterschool Programs.* Thousand Oaks, CA: Corwin, 2002.

Ferlazzo, Larry, and Lorrie A. Hammond. *Building Parent Engagement in Schools.* Santa Barbara, CA: ABC-CLIO, 2009.

Fleming, SJ, David L. *Draw Me into Your Friendship: The Spiritual Exercises.* Boston, MA: Institute of Jesuit Sources, 1996.

Fleming, SJ, David L. *Like the Lightning: The Dynamics of the Ignatian Exercises.* Boston, MA: Institute of Jesuit Sources, 2004.

Flynn, Gabriel, and Paul D. Murray. *Ressourcement: A Movement for Renewal in Twentieth Century Theology.* Oxford: Oxford University Press, 2014.

Foucault, Michel. *Power/Knowledge: Selected Interviews and Other Writings 1972–1977.* Cambridge, MA: Harvard University Press, 1980.

Freire, Paulo. *Pedagogy of the Oppressed.* New York: Bloomsbury Academics, 1970.

Freire, Paulo. *Teachers as Cultural Workers: Letters to Those Who Dare to Teach.* Boulder, CO: Westview Press, 2005.

Friedrich, Markus. *The Jesuits: A History.* Princeton, NJ: Princeton University Press, 2022.

Fullan, Michael. *The New Meaning of Educational Change.* New York: Teachers College Press, 2001.

Gadamer, Hans-Georg. *Truth and Method.* New York: Bloomsbury, 1960.

Gallagher, Timothy. *The Examen Prayer: Ignatian Wisdom for Our Lives Today.* Chestnut Ridge, NY: Crossroad, 2006.

Galtung, Johan. "Kultuerlle gewalt." *Der Burger im Staat* 43 (1993): 106.

Gamberini, Paulo. "Ignatian Spirituality and Anglican Ethos: A Family Resemblance." *One in Christ* 49 (2015): 2–21.

Gamberini, Paulo. "Anglicanism and Ignatian Spirituality." In *Ecumenism and Ignatian Spirituality: Proceedings of the 22nd International Congress of Jesuit Ecumenists*, edited by Robert J. Daly and T. Hughes, 119–44. Institute for Advanced Jesuit Studies, Boston College, 2016.

Gandhi, Mohandas K. *Mahatma Gandhi: The Essential Writings.* New York: Oxford University Press, 2008.

Ganss, George E. *Ignatius of Loyola: Selected Works and Spiritual Exercises.* Mahwah, NJ: Paulist Press, 1991.

Ganss, George E. *Ignatius of Loyola: The Spiritual Exercises.* Chicago, IL: Loyola Press, 1992.

Gardner, Howard. *Frames of Mind: Theories of Multiple Intelligences.* New York: Basic Books, 1985.

Garguilo, Richard M., and Debbie Metcalf. *Teaching in Today's Inclusive Classrooms: A Universal Design for Learning Approach.* Boston, MA: Cengage Learning, 2017.

Garrow, David J. *Bearing the Cross: Martin Luther King, Jr., and the Southern Christian Leadership Conference.* New York: Perennial Classics, 1999.

Geger, SJ, Barton T. "What *Magis* Really Means and Why It Matters." *Jesuit Higher Education* 1, no. 2 (2012): 16–31.

Geger, SJ, Barton T. (Ed.). *A Pilgrim's Testament: The Memoirs of Saint Ignatius of Loyola.* Boston, MA: Institute of Jesuit Sources, 2020.

Gilligan, James. *Violence: Reflections on a National Epidemic.* New York: Vintage Books, 1997.

Givens, Jarvis R. *Fugitive Pedagogy: Carter G. Woodson and the Art of Black Teaching.* Cambridge, MA: Harvard University Press, 2021.

Goldstein, Eda G. *Ego Psychology and Their Children: Research on the Family Life Cycle.* Washington, DC: American Psychological Association, 1995.

Goldstein, Eda G. *Ego Psychology and Social Work Practice.* New York: The Free Press, 1995.

González, Norma, Luis C. Moll, and Cathy Amani. *Funds of Knowledge: Theorizing Practice in Household, Communities and Practice.* New York: Routledge, 2006.

Groenhout, Ruth E. *Connected Lives: Human Nature and an Ethics of Care.* Washington, DC: Rowman & Littlefield, 2004.

Groome, Thomas H. *What Makes Education Catholic: Spiritual Foundations.* Maryknoll, NY: Orbis Books. 2021.

Guiliano, Zachary, and Charles M. Stang (Eds.). *The Open Body: Chapters in Anglican Ecclesiology.* Pieterlen, Switzerland: Peter Lang, 2012.

Gurain, Michael, and Kathy Stevens. *The Minds of Boys: Saving Our Sons from Falling Behind in School and Life.* San Francisco, CA: Jossey-Bass, 2005.

Hall, Radclyffe. *The Well of Loneliness.* Stellar Books, 1928/2013.

Halper, Robert, Sharon Deich, and Carol Cohen. *Financing After-school Programs.* The Finance Project, 2000.

Hammond, Zaretta. *Culturally Responsive Teaching and the /Brain: Promoting Authentic Engagement and Rigor among Culturally and Linguistically Diverse Students.* Thousand Oaks, CA: Corwin, 2014.

Harter, Michael G. *Hearts on Fire: Praying with Jesuits.* Boston, MA: Institute of Jesuit Sources, 1993.

Hatch, Thomas. "How Community Action Contributes to Achievement." *Educational Leadership* 55, no. 8 (1998): 16–19.

Hatch, Thomas. *The Education We Need for a Future We Can't Predict.* Thousand Oaks, CA: Corwin, 2021.

Hauerwas, Stanley. *A Community of Character: Toward a Constructive Christian Social Ethic.* Notre Dame, IN: University of Notre Dame Press, 1991.

Hendrickson, SJ, Daniel S. *Jesuit Higher Education in a Secular Age: A Response to Charles Taylor and the Crisis of Fullness.* Washington, DC: Georgetown University Press, 2022.

Heschel, Abraham Joshua. *Man Is Not Alone: A Philosophy of Religion.* New York: Farrar, Straus and Giroux, 1951.

Heschel, Abraham Joshua. *The Sabbath: Its Meaning for Modern Man.* New York: Farrar, Straus and Giroux, 1951.

Heschel, Abraham Joshua. *The Prophets: An Introduction, Vol. I.* New York: Harper Torchbooks, 1962.

Heschel, Abraham Joshua. *The Prophets, Vol. II.* New York: Harper Torchbooks, 1962.

Hill Fletcher, Jeannine. *Motherhood as Metaphor: Engendering Interreligious Dialogue.* Kindle Version. New York: Fordham University Press, 2013.

Hill Fletcher, Jeannine. *The Sin of White Supremacy: Christianity, Racism, and Religious Diversity in America.* Maryknoll, NY: Orbis Press, 2018.

Hitchens, Christopher. *God is Not Great: How Religion Poisons Everything*. New York: Twelve, 2009.

Hodge, David R. "Religious Discrimination and Ethical Compliance: Exploring Perceptions Among a Professionally Affiliated Sample of Graduate Students." *Journal of Religion and Spirituality in Social Work* 2 (2007): 91–113.

Horsch, K. *Indicators: Definition and Use in a Results-based Accountability System*. Cambridge, MA: Harvard Family Research Project, 1997.

Hugget, Joyce. "Why Ignatian Spirituality Hooks Protestants." *The Way* 68 (1990): 22–34.

Hull, Ernest R. *The Formation of Character*. St. Louis: B. Herder, 1921.

Ivens, Michael. *Understanding the Spiritual /Exercises: A Handbook for Retreat Directors*. Herefordshire: Gracewing Publishing, 2000.

Jackson, Yvette. *The Pedagogy of Confidence: Inspiring High Intellectual Performance in Urban Schools*. New York: Teachers College Press, 2011.

James, Richard K. *Crisis Intervention Strategies* (6th ed.). Belmont, CA: Thomson Brooks/Cole, 2008.

Jensen, Frances E. *The Teenage Brain: A Neuroscientist's Survival Guide to Raising Adolescents and Young Adults*. New York: Harper Collins, 2015.

Jesuit-Sponsored School. *Student and Family Handbook*. 2008–2009.

Jiménez-Castellanos, Oscar, Alberto M. Ochoa, and Edward M. Olivos. "Operationalizing Transformative Parent Engagement in Latino School Communities: A Case Study." *Journal of Latino/Latin American Studies* 8, no. 1 (2016): 93–107.

Johnson, Elizabeth A. *She Who Is: The Mystery of God in Feminist Theological Discourse*. Chestnut Ridge, NY: Crossroad, 1992.

Johnson, R. Burke. "Examining the Validity Structure of Qualitative Research." *Education* 118, no. 2 (1997, Winter): 282–92.

Jones, Cheryl Bridges. *Pentecostal Formation: A Pedagogy Among the Oppressed*. Eugene, OR: Wipf and Stock Press, 1998.

Jung, Carl G. *Psychology and Religion*. New Haven, CT: Yale University Press, 1966.

Jung, Carl G. *Encountering Christianity*. Princeton, NJ: Princeton University Press, 1999.

Katsouros, Steve N. *Come to Believe: How the Jesuits Are Reinventing Education (Again)*. Maryknoll, NY: Orbis Press, 2017.

Kendall, Mikki. *Hood/Feminism: Notes from the Women That a Movement Forgot*. New York: Viking, 2020.

Kennedy, William Bean. "Conversation with Paulo Freire." *Religious Education* 79, no. 4 (1984): 511–22.

Keyes, Corey L. M., and Jonathan Haidt (Eds.). *Flourishing: Positive Psychology and the Life Well-lived*. Washington, DC: American Psychological Association, 2003.

Kim, Johnny S., and Calvin L. Streeter. "Increasing School Attendance: Effective Strategies and Interventions." In *The School Services Sourcebook: A Guide for School-*

based Professionals, edited by Cynthia Franklin, Mary Beth Harris, and Paula Allen-Meares, 397–404. New York: Oxford University Press, 2006.

Kindlon, Dan, and Michael Thompson. *Raising Cain: Protecting the Emotional Life of Boys*. New York: Ballantine Trade Paperback, 1999.

Kirylo, James D. *The Thoughtful Teacher: Making Connections with a Diverse Student Population*. Washington, DC: Rowman & Littlefield, 2021.

Kohlberg, Lawrence. *The Philosophy of Moral Development: Moral Stages and the Idea of Justice (Essays on Moral Development, Vol. 1)*. New York: Harper and Row, 1981.

Kolbe, Kathy. *Pure Instinct: The M.O. of High Performance People and Teams*. Phoenix, AZ: Monumentus Press, 2004.

Kolvenbach, Peter-Hans. *Go Forth and Teach: The Characteristics of Jesuit Education*. Washington, DC: Jesuit Secondary Education Association Foundations, 1986.

Kralovec, Etta, and John Buell. "End Homework Now." *Educational Leadership* (2001, April): 39–42.

Langton, Rae. "Feminism in Epistemology: Exclusion and Objectification." In *The Cambridge Companion to Feminism in Philosophy*, edited by Miranda Fricker and Jennifer Hornsby, 127–45. Cambridge University Press, 2000.

Lazear, David. *Seven Pathways of Learning: Teaching Students and Parents About Multiple Intelligences*. Brookline, MA: Zephyr Press, 1994.

LeCompte, Margaret D., and Jean J. Schensul. *Designing and Conducting Ethnographic Research: An Introduction*. Walnut Creek, CA: AltaMira Press, 2010.

Lee, Harper. *To Kill a Mockingbird*. Philadelphia, PA: J. B. Lippincott & Co., 1960.

Lee, Othelia Eun-Kyoung, and Callan Barrett. "Integrating Spirituality, Faith, and Social Justice in Social Work Practice and Education: A Pilot Study." *Journal of Religion and Spirituality in Social Work* 2 (2007): 1–21.

Levin, Henry. *Privatizing Education: Can the Marketplace Deliver Choice, Efficiency, Equity, and Social Cohesion?* Boulder, CO: Westview Press, 2001.

Lonergan, Bernard. *Insight: A Study of Human Understanding, 3*. Toronto: University of Toronto Press, 1992.

Loyola, Ignatius. *Letters and Instructions*. Boston, MA: Institute of Jesuit Sources, 2006.

Luke, Carmen. *Pedagogy, Printing and Protestantism: The Discourse on Childhood*. Albany, NY: State University of New York Press, 1989.

Luke, Carmen, and Jennifer Gore. *Feminisms and Critical Pedagogy*. New York: Routledge, 1992.

Mackinnon, Catharine A. *Feminism Unmodified: Discourses on Life and Law*. Cambridge, MA: Harvard University Press, 1988.

Maher, Frances A. "Classroom Pedagogy and the New Scholarship on Women." In *Gendered Subjects: The Dynamics of Feminist Teaching*, edited by Margo Culley and Catherine Portuge, 29–48. New York: Routledge and Kegan Paul, 1985.

Maher, Frances A. "Inquiry Teaching and Feminist Pedagogy." *Social Education* 51, no. 3 (1987): 186–92.

Mahoney, Joseph L., Reed W. Larson, Jacquelynne S. Eccles, and Heather Lord. "Organized Activities as Developmental Contexts for Children and Adolescents." In *Organized Activities as Contexts of Development: Extracurricular Activities, After-school and Community Programs*, edited by Joseph L. Mahoney, Reed W. Larson, and Jacquelynne S. Eccles, 3–22. Mahwah, NJ: Lawrence Erlbaum, 2005.

Mann, Horace, and Mary Tyler Peabody Mann. *Life and Works of Horace Mann*, vol. 1. RareBooksClub.com, 2012.

Marable, Manning. "The Black Male: Searching Beyond Stereotypes." In *Men's Lives* (5th ed.), edited by M. S. Kimmel and M. A. Messner, 17–23. Boston, MA: Allyn & Bacon, 2001.

March, Artemis et al. "Radicalesbians." In *The Woman-Identified Woman*. Second Congress to Unite Women, 1970. The Woman-Identified Woman/Women's Liberation Movement Print Culture/Duke Digital Repository.

Marger, Martin N. (Ed.). *Race and Ethnic Relations: American and Global Perspective* (10th ed.). Boston, MA: Cengage Learning, 2015.

Marion Young, Iris. *Justice and the Politics of Difference*. Princeton, NJ: Princeton University Press, 2011.

Marsiglia, Flavio Francisco, and Stephen Kulis. *Diversity, Oppression and Change* (2nd ed.). Houston, TX: Lyceum Books, 2015.

Marsiglia, Flavio Francisco, Stephen Kulis, and Stephanie Lechuga-Peña. "The Intersectionality of Race and Ethnicity with Other Factors." In *Diversity, Oppression, and Change: Culturally Grounded Social Work* (2nd ed.), 52–72. Houston, TX: Lyceum Books, 2015.

Maxwell, Joseph A. *Qualitative Research Design: An Interactive Approach*. Thousand Oaks, CA: Sage, 1996.

Mazor, Aviva. "Same-gender Couple/Therapy: Creating New Objects in Intimacy and Parenthood Transition." *Contemporary Family Therapy* 26, no. 4 (2004): 409–23.

McGreevy, John T. *Catholicism: A Global History from the French Revolution to Pope Francis*. New York: W. W. Norton & Company, 2022.

McGucken, William J. *The Jesuits and Education: The Society's Teaching Principles and Practice*. Eugene, OR: Wipf and Stock, 2008.

Merton, Robert K., George G. Reader, and Patricia Kendall (Eds.). *The Student Physician*. Cambridge, MA: Harvard University Press, 1957.

Messer, Neil. *Flourishing: Health, Disease and Bioethics in Theological Perspective*. Grand Rapids, MI: William Eerdmans, 2013.

Metts, Ralph E. *Ignatius Knew*. Washington, DC: Jesuit Secondary Education Association, 1995.

Miller, Beth M. "The Promise of After-school Programs." *Educational Leadership* (2001, April): 6–12.

Miller, Lisa. *The Awakened Brain: The New Science of Spirituality and Our Quest for the Inspired Life*. New York: Random House, 2021.

Modras, Ronald. *Ignatian Humanism: A Dynamic Spirituality for the Twenty-First Century*. Loyola Press, 2004.

Monette, Duane E., Thomas J. Sullivan, and Cornel R. DeJong. *Applied Social Research: A Tool for the Human Services*. Thomson Wadsworth, 2008.

Morgan, Joan. *When the Chickenheads Come Home to Roost: A Hip-Hop Feminist Breaks It Down*. New York: Simon and Schuster, 2017.

Morrell, Ernest, Rudy Duenas, Veronica Garcia-Garza, and Jorge Lopez, J. *Critical Media Pedagogy: Teaching for Achievement in City Schools*. New York: Teachers College Press, 2013.

Morse, Jennifer Roback. "No Families, No Freedom: Human Flourishing in a Free Society." In *Human Flourishing*, edited by Ellen Frankel Paul, Fred D. Miller, and Jeffrey Paul, 290–314. Cambridge University Press, 2013.

Morton-Young, Tommie. *After-School and Parent Education Programs for At-Risk Youth and Their Families: A Guide to Organizing and Operating a Community-Based Center for Basic Educational Skills Reinforcement, Homework Assistance, Cultural Enrichment, and a Parent Involvement Focus*. Springfield, IL: Charles C. Thomas, 1995.

Muhammad, Gholdy. *Cultivating Genius: An Equity Framework for Culturally and Historically Responsive Literacy*. New York: Scholastic, 2020.

Muoneme, Maduabuchi Leo. *The Hermeneutics of Jesuit Leadership in Higher Education: The Meaning and Culture of Jesuit-Catholic Presidents*. New York: Routledge, 2017.

Myers, JoAnne. *The Good Citizen: The Markers of Privilege in America*. New York: Routledge, 2020.

Nicole Brown, Ruth, and Chamara Jewel Kwakye. (2012). *Wish to Live: The Hip Hop Feminism Pedagogy Reader*. Pieterlen, Switzerland: Peter Lang, 2012.

Noam, Gil G., Gina Biancarosa, and Nadine Dechausay. *Afterschool Education: Approaches to an Emerging Field*. Cambridge, MA: Harvard Education Press, 2003.

Noam, Gil G., and Nina Fiore. "Relationships Across Multiple Settings: An Overview." *New Directions for Youth Development* (2004): 9–16.

Noam, Gil G., B. M. Miller, and S. Barry. "Youth Development and Afterschool Time: Policy and Programming in Large Cities." *New Directions for Youth Development* (2002): 9–18.

Noam, Gil G., and J. Rosenbaum Tillinger. "After-School as Intermediary Space: Theory and Typology of Partnerships." *New Directions for Youth Development* (2004): 75–113.

Nussbaum, Martha C. *Hiding from Humanity: Disgust, Shame, and the Law*. Princeton, NJ: Princeton University Press, 2004.

Nussbaum, Martha C. *Creating Capabilities: The Human Development Approach*. Cambridge, MA: Belknap Press, 2013.

O'Malley, John W. *The First Jesuits*. Cambridge, MA: Harvard University Press, 1993.

O'Malley, John W. *Four Cultures of the West*. Cambridge, MA: The Belknap Press of Harvard University Press, 2004.

Palmer, Martin E. *On Giving the Spiritual Exercises: The Early Jesuit Manuscript Directories and the Official Directory of 1599*. Boston, MA: Institute of Jesuit Sources, 1996.

Paul, Ellen Frankel, Fred D. Miller, Jr., and Jeffrey Paul (Eds.). *Human Flourishing*. Cambridge: Cambridge University Press, 1999.

Pavur, SJ, Claude. *The Ratio Studiorum: The Official Plan for Jesuit Education*. Boston, MA: Institute of Jesuit Sources, 2005.

Pavur, SJ, Claude. *In the School of Ignatius: Studious Zeal and Devoted Learning*. Boston, MA: Institute of Jesuit Sources, 2019.

Peters, Laurence. *Creating the Global Classroom: Approaches to Developing the Next Generation of World Savvy Students*. New York: Routledge, 2022.

Peters, Richard Stanley. *Ethics and Education*. New South Wales: George Allen and Unwin, 1986.

Peterson, Christopher, and Seligman, Martin E. P. *Character Strengths and Virtues: A Handbook and Classification*. New York: Oxford University Press, 2004.

Phelan, Shane. *Gays, Lesbians and Dilemmas of Citizenship*. Philadelphia, PA: Temple University Press, 2001.

Piers, Gerhart, and Milton B. Singer. *Shame and Guilt: A Psychoanalytic and a Cultural Study*. New York: W. W. Norton, 1971.

Pollack, William. *Real Boys: Rescuing Our Sons from the Myths of Boyhood*. New York: Random House, 1998.

Probyn, Elspeth. *Blush: Faces of Shame*. Minneapolis, MN: University of Minnesota Press, 2005.

Radd, Sharon I., Gretchen Givens Generett, Mark Anthony Gooden, and George Theoharis. "Practices and Policies for Out-of-School Time." In *Organized Activities as Contexts of Development: Extracurricular Activities, After-school and Community Programs*, edited by Joseph Mahoney, Reed W. Larson, and Jacquelynne S. Eccles, 479–95. Mahwah, NJ: Lawrence Erlbaum, 2005.

Radd, Sharon I., Gretchen Givens Generett, Mark Anthony Gooden, and George Theoharis (Eds.). *Five Practices for Equity-Focused School Leadership*. Alexandria, VA: ASCD, 2021.

Rahner, Karl. *Spiritual Exercises*. New York: Herder and Herder, 1965.

Roberts, Robert W., and Robert H. Nee (Eds.). *Theories of Social Casework*. Chicago, IL: University of Chicago Press, 1970.

Roccasalvo, J. L. *Prayer for Finding God in All Things: The Daily Examen of St. Ignatius Loyola*. Boston, MA: Institute of Jesuit Sources, 2005.

Rorty, Richard. *Achieving Our Country*. Cambridge, MA: Harvard University Press, 1998.

Rossi, Peter H., Mark W. Lipsey, and Howard E. Freeman. *Evaluation: A Systematic Approach* (7th ed.). Thousand Oaks, CA: Sage, 2004.

Rothenberg, Paula S. (Ed.). *Race, Class, and /Gender in the United States: An Integrated Study* (10th ed.). New York: Worth Publishers, 2017.

Sadovnik, Alan, Peter Cookson, and Susan Semel. *Exploring Education: An Introduction to the Foundations of Education*. Boston, MA: Allyn and Bacon, 2001.

Sameroff, A. J., and L. M. Gutman. "Contributions of Risk Research to the Design of Successful Interventions." In *Intervention with Children and Adolescents: An Interdisciplinary Perspective*, edited by Paula Allen-Meares and Mark W. Fraser, 9–26. San Francisco, CA: Pearson Education, 2004.

Santamaria, Lorri J., and Andrés Santamaria. *Applied Critical Leadership in Education: Choosing Change*. New York: Routledge, 2012.

Schussler-Fiorenza, Elisabeth. *Wisdom Ways: Introducing Feminist Biblical Interpretation*. Maryknoll, NY: Orbis Press, 2001.

Schussler-Fiorenza, Elisabeth. *Congress of Wo/men: Religion, Gender and Kyriarchal power*. Cambridge: Feminist Studies in Religion, 2017.

Schwickerath, Robert. *Jesuit Education: Its History and Principles Viewed in the Light of Modern Education Problems*. St. Louis: B. Herder, 1903.

SEDL Letter. *Afterschool, Family, and Community* 20, no. 2 (2008, August).

Seider, Scott. *Character Compass: How Powerful School Culture Can Point Students Toward Success*. Cambridge, MA: Harvard University Press, 2015.

Sen, Amartya. *Development as Freedom*. New York: Anchor Books, 2011.

Senge, Peter, Nelda Cambron-McCabe, Timothy Lucas, Bryan Smith, Janis Dutton, and Art Kleiner (Eds.). *Schools That Learn: A Fifth Discipline Fieldbook for Educators, Parents, and Everyone Who Cares about Education*. New York: Crown Business, 2012.

Shirley, Betsy. "The Era of the Parochial School Is Over. Meet the Catholic Educators Searching for What's Next." *America Magazine* (2019). www.americamagazine.org

Sibilla, Nick. "The Court Case That Could Finally Take Down Antiquated Anti-Catholic Laws." *The Atlantic* (2020). www.theatlantic.com

Slocumb, Paul D. *Hear Our Cry: Boys in Crisis*. Aha! Process, 2007.

Smarick, Andy, and Kelly Robson. "Catholic School Renaissance: A Wise Giver's Guide to Strengthening a National Asset." *Philosophy Roundtable* (2015). www.philosophyround table.org

Society of Jesus. *Ignatian Pedagogy: Practical Approach*. Rome, Italy, 1993.

Sommers, Christina Hoff. *The War Against Boys: How Misguided Feminism Is Harming Our Young Men*. New York: Simon & Schuster, 2000.

Steen, Julie A. "The Roots of Human Rights Advocacy and a Call to Action." *Social Work* 51, no. 2 (2006): 101–6.

Stevenson, Bryan. *Just Mercy: A Story of Justice and Redemption*. London: Oneworld Publications, 2015.

Swaner, Lynn E., and Andy Wolfe. *Flourishing Together: A Christian Vision for Students, Educators, and Schools*. Grand Rapids, MI: William B. Eerdmans, 2021.

Taylor, Charles. "Cognitive Psychology." In *Human Agency and Language (Philosophical Papers), Vol. 1*, 187–212. Cambridge, MA: Harvard University Press, 1985.

Taylor, Charles. *Sources of the Self: The Making of Modern Identity*. Cambridge, MA: Harvard University Press, 1992.

Taylor, Carol R., and Roberto Dell'Oro (Eds.). *Health and Human Flourishing.* Washington, DC: Georgetown University Press, 2006.

Tetlow, Joseph A. *Choosing Christ in the World: A Handbook for Directing the Spiritual Exercises of St. Ignatius Loyola According to Annotations Eighteen and Nineteen.* Boston, MA: Institute of Jesuit Sources, 1999.

Thatamanil, John J., and Cornel West. *Ghandi and King Class Lecture Notes.* Union Theological Seminary, New York, April 14, 2015.

Thibodeaux, SJ, Mark E. *Armchair Mystic: Easing into Contemplative Prayer.* Cincinnati: St. Anthony Messenger Press, 2001.

Thomas, Laurence. *Living Morally: A Psychology of Moral Character.* Philadelphia, PA: Temple University Press, 1989.

Tong, Rosemarie. *Feminist Thought: A More Comprehensive Introduction.* Boulder, CO: Westview Press, 2009.

Traub, George W. *A Jesuit Education Reader.* Chicago, IL: Loyola Press, 2008.

Tuana, Nancy. *Woman and the History of Philosophy.* New York: Paragon Press, 1992.

Tyack, David, and Larry Cuban. *Tinkering Toward Utopia: A Century of Public School Reform.* Cambridge, MA: Harvard University Press, 1995.

Tyack, David, and W. Tobin. "The 'Grammar' of Schooling: Why Has It Been So Hard to Change?" *American Education Research Journal* 31, no. 3 (1994): 453–79.

Tylenda, SJ, Joseph N. *A Pilgrim's Journey: The Autobiography of Ignatius of Loyola.* San Francisco, CA: Ignatius Press, 2001.

Urdang, Esther. *Human Behavior in the Social Environment: Interweaving the Inner and Outer Worlds.* The Haworth Social Work Practice Press, 2015.

Villa, Richard A., and Jacqueline S. Thousand. *Creating an Inclusive School.* Alexandria, VA: ASCD, 2005.

Villa, Richard A., and Jacqueline S. Thousand. *Leading an Inclusive School: Access and Success for All Students.* Alexandria, VA: ASCD, 2017.

von Drehle, David. "The Boys Are All Right." *Time* (2007, August 6): 39–47.

Walch, Timothy. *Parish School: American Catholic Parochial Education from Colonial Times to the present.* Leesburg, VA: National Catholic Education Association (NCEA), 2016.

Walsh, Michael. *From Ignatius to Francis: The Jesuits in History.* Collegeville, MN: Liturgical Press Academic, 2022.

Washington, James Melvin (Ed.). *A Testament of Hope: The Essential Writings and Speeches of Martin Luther King, Jr.* San Francisco, CA: Harper San Francisco, 1991.

Way, N., and J. Y. Chu (Eds.). *Adolescent Boys: Exploring Diverse Cultures of Boyhood.* New York: New York University Press, 2004.

Weeks, Jeffrey. *Against Nature: Chapters on History, Sexuality and Identity.* London: Rivers Oram Press, 1991.

Weissberg, Roger P., Karol L. Kumpfer, and Martin E. P. Seligman. "Prevention That Works for Children and Youth: An Introduction." *American Psychologist* 58 (2003, June/July): 425–32.

West, Cornel. *Race Matters*. New York: Vintage, 1994.
West, Cornel (Ed.). *The Radical King*. Boston, MA: Beacon Press, 2015.
Wong, Harry K., and Rosemary T. Wong. *The First Days of School: How to be an Effective Teacher*. (5th ed.). Mountain View, CA: Harry K. Wong Publications, 2018.
Wordsworth, William. *The Collected Poems of William Wordsworth*. Digireads, 2018.
Yancy, George (Ed.). *What White Looks Like: African-American Philosophers on the Whiteness Question*. New York: Routledge, 2004.
Yarbough, Denise. "Radical Hospitality: Interreligious Dialogue as Christian Mission in the Twenty-first Century." In *The Open Body: Chapters in Anglican Ecclesiology*, edited by Zachary Guiliano and Charles M. Stang. Pieterlen, Switzerland: Peter Lang, 2012.
Young, Ellie L., Paul Caldarella, Michael J. Richardson, and K. Richard Young (Eds.). *Positive Behavior Support in Secondary Schools: A Practical Guide*. New York: The Guilford Press, 2012.
Young, Iris. "Five Faces of Oppression." In *Oppression, Privilege, and Resistance*, edited by Lisa Heldke and Peg O'Connor, 37–63. New York: McGraw-Hill, 2004.
Zief, Susan Goerlich, Sherri Lauver, and Rebecca A. Maynard. *Impacts of After-school Programs on Student Outcomes: A Systematic Review for the Campbell Collaboration* (2006). www.sfi.dk/graphics/ Campbell/reviews/afterschool_review.pdf

Annotated Bibliography

I have organized this annotated bibliography to assist readers with additional learning about Ignatian Pedagogy, Jesuit education, and the spirituality of the Society of Jesus. I present the texts in a self-determined order of importance, therefore the texts are not organized alphabetically but rather in a way that encourages readers and researchers to work their own way through these texts.

A. Historical (Including Primary Sources) (from Founding of Society in 1540 to the Twenty-First Century)

This section is important because it evidences the thought of St. Ignatius of Loyola, the founder of the Jesuits (Society of Jesus) and his first companions. It also evidences the historical organization of the Jesuits and demonstrates the sociocultural context through which the Jesuits aim to deliver services, for example, education, retreats, and missionary work. Such work is aimed at bringing people closer to God, and thereby to increase people's human flourishing.

1. Ignatius of Loyola—*Letters, Autobiography, and Spiritual Exercises* (Primary Source)

This book is important because it includes primary source documents, including Ignatius's letters. The letters detail the formation of the Jesuits and concerns of Ignatius and are helpful for knowing the mindset of Ignatius.

2. Ribadeneira—*Life of Ignatius* (Primary Source)

This book is important because it is the first official biography of Ignatius. The author is an early companion of Ignatius.

3. Palmer—*On Giving the Spiritual Exercises: The /Early Jesuit Manuscript Directories and the Official Directory of 1599* (1996)

This book is important because it includes Ignatius's own remarks about directing the Exercises.

4. Modras—*Ignatian Humanism* (2004)

This book is important because it shows the development and relevance of Ignatian Spirituality over time. It includes topics on Matteo Ricci, Friedrich Spee, Karl Rahner, Pierre Teilhard de Chardin, and Pedro Arrupe.

5. Costelloe—*The Letters and Writings of St. Francis Xavier* (Primary Source)

This book is important because it provides insight into the companionship between Xavier and Ignatius. It provides examples of how Ignatian Spirituality and the Jesuits shaped and interacted with new cultures.

6. Murphy and Palmer—*Spiritual Writings of Peter Faber* (Primary Source)

This book is important because Faber is considered the saint of the Exercises. Ignatius considered him the best director of the Exercises.

7. de Camara—*Remembering Iñigo: Glimpses of the Life of Saint Ignatius of Loyola: The Memoriale of Luís Gonçalves da Cámara* (Primary Source)

This book is important because it includes material that became part of Ignatius's earliest autobiography. It offers insight into Ignatius's humanity.

8. Divarkar—*A Pilgrim's Testament: The Memoirs of Saint Ignatius of Loyola* (Primary Source)

This book is important because it tells the founder of the Jesuits testament and provides his paternal instruction, and offers insight into God's guiding of Ignatius through his conversion.

9. *The Constitutions and Complementary Norms of the Society of Jesus* (Primary Source)

This book is important because it represents the spirit of the Society of Jesus and its organization and indicates how the Jesuits are to live out their spirituality and who Jesuits are to be.

10. O'Malley—*The First Jesuits* (1995)

This book is important because it is considered the seminal text of the founding of the Society of Jesus.

11. O'Malley—*The Jesuits: A History from Ignatius to the Present* (2014)

This book is important because it looks linearly at the Jesuits through history and now offers new material on Pope Francis I.

12. Ganss—*The Jesuits: Their Spiritual Doctrine and Practice: A Historical Study* (1964)

This book is important because it looks at Jesuit Spirituality through the hermeneutic of a mystical Ignatius of Loyola, and also looks at controversies in the Jesuit order through the twentieth century and the doctrine and practices in the history of Jesuit Spirituality.

13. O'Malley—*The Jesuits: Cultures, Sciences and the Arts, 1540-1773* (Volume I and II) (2015)

These books are important because they offer insights into the suppression of the Jesuits, with attention paid to how the Jesuits shaped the development of communities by the Society of Jesus.

14. Burson—*The Jesuit Suppression in Global Context: Causes, Events, and Consequences* (2015)

This book is important because it reflects the complex international elements of the Society of Jesus.

15. Cordara—*On the Suppression of the Society of Jesus* (1999)

This book is important because it is the firsthand account of the suppression of the Society of Jesus.

16. Battista Nicolini—*History of the Jesuits: Their Origin, Progress, Doctrines, and Designs* (2012)

This book is important because it discusses the origin, progress, doctrine, and designs of the Jesuits.

17. Costello—*From Inspiration to Invention: Rhetoric in the Constitution of the Society of Jesus* (2011)

This book is important because it offers a fresh look at the spirituality of the Constitutions of the Society of Jesus. Connections between the rules of Basil, Augustine, Benedict, and Francis are offered.

18. Bangert—*A History of the Society of Jesus* (1986)

This book is important because it is the most comprehensive history of the Jesuits. It includes the author's chronological views to the changing ecclesiology, political, social, and cultural contexts of the Society of Jesus.

19. *Reports and Findings of the General Congregations of the Society of Jesus* (Primary Source)

These documents are primary source documents that demonstrate the mission, vision, and prayer of the Society of Jesus. These documents reveal how the Society of Jesus shapes its organization and planning around contemporary and pressing issues, for example, climate change and fewer Jesuits.

20. Tylenda—*A Pilgrim's Journey: The Autobiography of Saint Ignatius of Loyola* (2001)

This book presents the earliest autobiography of Ignatius as told by the founder of the Jesuits to de Camara at the request of his close associates Polanco and Nadal.

B. Mystical and Theological (Twentieth and Twenty-First Centuries)

This section is important because it situates the Spiritual Exercises of Ignatius of Loyola in its mystical and theological roots. These works address Ignatius's incarnational theology, reveal his mysticism, and treat the Spiritual Exercises through the lens of their contribution to the person's human flourishing in God. These texts interpret Ignatius's various Exercises, meditations, and contemplations through the lens of theology and make connections to scripture, for example, Hebrew and Christian Testaments.

1. H. Rahner—*Ignatius the Theologian* (1991)

This book is important because Rahner develops Ignatius's remarkable theology, founded on perceiving God in prayer.

2. Coutinho—*An Ignatian Pathway: Experiencing the Mystical Dimension of the Spiritual Exercises* (2011)

This book is important because it helps readers enter the mysticism of the Exercises. It is a companion piece to the Exercises.

3. K. Rahner—*Spiritual Exercises* (1967)

This book is important because it lays out Rahner's theological foundations of the Exercises. It was completed by one of the greatest theologians in the church.

4. Thibodeuax—*Armchair Mystic: Easing into Contemplative Prayer* (2001)

This book is important because it teaches prayers how to ease into the mystical prayer of Ignatius. The author sees these stages as evidence of maturation of prayer: talking at God, talking to God, listening to God, and being with God.

5. Segundo—*The Christ of the Ignatian Exercises* (1987)

This book is important because it examines the place of Jesus the Christ in the four-week model of the Exercises.

6. Lonergan—*The Dynamism of Desire* (on Ignatius's Spiritual Exercises) (2006)

This book is important because Lonergan's cognitional theory/theology (experience, inquiry and understanding, judgment, and decision-making) is used to analyze and evaluate the theology of Ignatius. Lonergan proposes an isomorphism between his cognitional theory and the strategy of the Exercises.

7. Cusson—*Experience of God as Accomplishing Within Us His Plan of Salvation* (1988) and *Spiritual Exercises Made in Everyday Life: A Method and a Biblical Interpretation* (1988)

These books are important because they look at the relationship between St. Paul and Ignatius. Cusson locates Ignatius's theology in God's plan of salvation for human beings as presented in the Scriptures.

8. H. Rahner—*The Vision of Ignatius in the Chapel of La Storta* (1979)

This book is important because it ponders Ignatius's mystical experience in the Chapel of La Storta.

9. Rupnik—*Human Frailty, Divine Redemption: The Theology and Practice of the Examen* (2012)

This book is important because the author explores these theological truths of prayer, our call to union with Christ, the place of memory in life-giving relationships, the effect of sin and sinfulness on relationships, the power of the redemption in our life, union with the three Persons of the Trinity, and our need to discover that we are loved.

C. Spiritual Exercises and the Ignatian Retreat (From Founding of Society of Jesus in 1540 through Twenty-First Century)

These texts represent different versions of the Spiritual Exercises, for example, the traditional "thirty-day" retreat, the eighteenth and nineteenth Annotations (aka retreats in everyday life). These texts are used as maps or guidebooks for retreatants who desire to pursue greater intimacy with God, to enhance their human flourishing, for example, to improve their relationships with God, self, and others. Such works provide data about the various Exercises, meditations, and contemplations that Ignatius proposed as helps and directions for retreatants.

1. Fleming—*Draw Me into Your Friendship: The Spiritual Exercises* (1996)

This book is important because it offers a literal and contemporary translation of the Exercises. I used this text in my own retreat and when directing people through the retreat. I have also used it in parish settings and for days of prayer with students.

2. Fleming—*Like the Lightning: The Dynamics of the Ignatian Exercises* (2004)

This book is important because it offers a commentary on the movements of the Exercises, specifically looking at the four weeks of the Exercises and specific meditations, contemplations, and Exercises.

3. Mariani—*Thirty Days: On Retreat with the Exercises of Ignatius* (2002)

This book is important because it is a memoir of a leading scholar of Gerard Manley Hopkins. It speaks about introspection, self-revelation, and spiritual renewal.

4. Ivens—*Understanding the Spiritual Exercises and Ivens—The Spiritual Exercises of Saint Ignatius of Loyola* (Companion Volumes) (2000 and 2004)

These books are important because they unravel the inner workings of the Exercises and go hand in hand with the author's translation of the Exercises.

5. Tetlow—*Making Choices in Christ: Foundations of Ignatian Spirituality* (2008)

This book is important because it speaks to discernment and how to discern God's will by using the tools of Ignatian Spirituality.

6. O'Brien—*The Ignatian Adventure: Experiencing the Spiritual Exercises of Ignatius Loyola in Daily Life* (2011)

This book is important because it connects Ignatian Spirituality to faith and everyday life. The book offers thirty-two weeks of prayer and meditations, speaking especially to the personal encounter with God.

7. Tetlow—*Choosing Christ in the World* (Nineteenth Annotation) (2000)

This book is important because it is the seminal text of the nineteenth Annotation with supplemental material. It is an aid for spiritual directors.

8. Toner—*Discerning God's Will: Ignatius of Loyola's Teaching on Christian Decision Making* (1991)

This book is important because it addresses the call to seek God, to find God in all things. The book defines spiritual consolation and desolation. It looks at freedom, indifference, and decision-making in Christian life.

9. Toner—*A Commentary on Saint Ignatius's Rules for the Discernment of Spirits: A Guide to the Principles and Practice* (1982)

This book is important because it evaluates difficult texts and treats controversial issues associated with discernment, for example, the existence of created spirits.

10. Aschenbrenner—*Stretched for Greater Glory: What to Expect from the Spiritual Exercises* (2004)

This book is important because it provides a sense of relevance to the Exercises for modernity. Theology is attached to human experience.

11. Sheldrake—*The Way of Ignatius Loyola: Contemporary Approaches to the Spiritual Exercises* (1991)

This book is important because it provides the main elements of the Sp. Ex. Text and includes a practical commentary on the dynamics of the Exercises. Twenty chapters provide various commentary.

12. Murphy—*The Spiritual Writings of Pierre Favre* (1996)

This book is important because it details the writings of Pierre Favre, the man Ignatius saw as the mystic of the Exercises, the best director of the retreat.

13. Fleming—*Notes on the Spiritual Exercises of Ignatius of Loyola* (1983)

This book is important because the thirty-nine chapters in this text treat Ignatian Spirituality in comprehensive and different ways.

14. Buelta—*Psalms to Accompany the Spiritual Exercises of St. Ignatius Loyola* (2012)

This book is important because it is a collection of a series of contemporary psalms, personal meditations born of the author's prayer, a life's journey with the Spiritual Exercises of St. Ignatius Loyola.

D. Ignatian Spirituality (Twentieth and Twenty-First Centuries)

This section exemplifies the Western desire for Ignatian Spirituality and includes works that attempt to make Ignatian Spirituality and the Spiritual

Exercises readily available for men and women who seek to flourish in relationship to God. This section is important because it demonstrates the response of Jesuits and lay people trained in Ignatian Spirituality who seek to maintain the vibrancy and vitality of Ignatian Spirituality as the number of Jesuits declines worldwide.

1. Lonsdale—*Eyes to See, Ears to Hear: Introduction to Ignatian Spirituality* (2000)

This book is important because Lonsdale argues about the primacy of discernment in the life of the Christian.

2. Martin—*The Jesuit Guide to Almost Everything* (2012)

This book is important because Marin is the second most famous Jesuit in the world; this text demonstrates the influence of Ignatian Spirituality on younger Roman Catholics.

3. English—*Spiritual Freedom: From an Experience of the Ignatian Exercises to the Art of Spiritual Guidance* (1995)

This book is important because it examines the place of freedom in Ignatian Spirituality. English provides meditations of the Spiritual Exercises and helps spiritual counselors develop a deeper understanding of the fundamental principles in the Exercises.

4. Kolvenbach—*The Road from La Storta: Peter-Hans Kolvenbach, SJ, on Ignatian Spirituality* (2000)

The Road from La Storta is a collection of twenty chapters by Peter-Hans Kolvenbach, former Superior General of the Society of Jesus, about the mission of the Jesuits. This book is important because he challenges Jesuits, and all followers of Ignatius, to consider this mission, which he examines from spiritual, analytical, and socio-pastoral perspectives.

5. Fagin—*Putting on the Heart of Christ* (2010)

This book is important because it looks at the Exercises through the lens of virtue ethics. Fagin explores fifteen virtues throughout the book, including gratitude, reverence, and forgiveness and treats them through the context of the Spiritual Exercises.

6. Au—*By Way of the Heart: Toward a Holistic Christian Spirituality* (1991)

This book is important because it is written by an ex-Jesuit who is also a psychologist. Au recommends an embodied spirituality of gospel values.

7. Hughes— *God of Surprises* (2008)

This book is important because the author analyzes the Kingdom of God through the Spiritual Exercises. The book also treats the human person's relationship with the institutional church.

8. Barry—*Finding God in All Things* (2009)

This book is important because it treats one of the most important themes of the Jesuit prayer, the examination of conscience, finding God in all things.

9. Barry—*Contemplatives in Action* (2005)

This book is important because it also treats a key piece of Ignatian Spirituality—being a contemplative in action. Such material is important for its connection to the corporal and spiritual works of mercy.

10. Silf—*Landmarks: Explorations in Ignatian Spirituality* (1998)

This book is important because it is one of the few on Ignatian Spirituality written by a woman. A practical book that helps readers discover and deepen their own spiritual journeys.

11. Gallagher—*Discernment of Spirits: An Ignatian Guide for Everyday Living* (2005)

This book is important because it is written by an Oblate of Mary. The book presents Ignatius's rules for the discernment of spirits and aids readers in implementing them in their everyday life.

12. Blackie—*Rooted in Love: Integrating Ignatian Spirituality into Daily Life* (2013)

This book is important because it is another text by a woman. It offers a blend of life experience and the principles of Ignatian Spirituality.

13. Gallagher—*Discerning the Will of God: An Ignatian Guide to Christian Decision Making* (2009)

This book is important because Gallagher steeps Christian decision-making in vocation and living a full life in God. It is countercultural today to live one's life according to God's will.

14. Gallagher—*The Examen Prayer: Ignatian Wisdom for Our Lives Today* (2006)

This book is important because it is a commentary and step-by-step guide to practicing the Examination of Conscience.

15. Silf—*Inner Compass: An Invitation to Ignatian Spirituality* (2007)

This book is important because it is in its tenth anniversary. The revised text includes a new introduction and personal invitation to the reader, a greatly expanded resource section, and a new design aimed at a new generation of spiritual readers.

16. Thibodeaux—*God's Voice Within: The Ignatian Way to Discover God's Will* (2010)

This book is important because it teaches readers how to become prayers. It helps them to discover God's will for them and that God works from within us.

17. Fleming—*What Is Ignatian Spirituality?* (2008)

This book is important because Fleming is a master of Ignatian Spirituality. He writes in his text that "God who loves us creates us and wants to share life with us forever. Our love response takes shape in our praise and honor and service of the God of our life." Fleming presents Ignatius's life vision, work vision, and vision of love.

18. Healey—*The Ignatian Way: Key Aspects of Jesuit Spirituality* (2009)

This book is important because it treats Ignatian Spirituality through the lens of its relationship to the founders of other religious orders.

19. Lowney—*Heroic Leadership (Ignatius and Corporate World)* (2005)

This book is important because it demonstrates why people seek out Ignatian formation, which transforms cultures and people—it suggests that the Jesuits shape culture.

20. Sheldrake—*Spirituality and History: Questions of Interpretation and Method* (1998)

This book is important because the author does not just take spiritual traditions at face value but attempts to uncover the cultural and socially defined questions that were being posed. He does this as a Jesuit informed by Ignatian Spirituality.

21. Wakefield—*Sacred Listening: Discovering the Spiritual Exercises of Ignatius Loyola* (2006)

This book is important because it looks at the place of the Exercises in non-Catholic traditions. The author examines the profound gift of God's mercy and forgiveness, the goals and values exemplified in the humanity of Christ and the price of redemption, and the cost of discipleship. Discipleship produces a new depth and richness in one's relationship with Christ.

22. Kane—*Building the Human City: William F. Lynch's Ignatian Spirituality for Public Life* (2016)

Fr. William Lynch, SJ, used Ignatian Spirituality to warn against polarization in culture and political life. Lynch believed that components of Ignatian Spirituality, for example, healing discernments and the transformation of sensibilities (artistic, intellectual) to promote change and transformation of society. The three purposes of the book are: (a) to cultivate society, (b) to remember William Lynch's contributions to the field of teaching and learning, and (c) to introduce readers to a spirituality that is both "thoroughly religious and appropriately secular" (see p. xiii).

23. Dyckman et al.—*The Spiritual Exercises Reclaimed: Uncovering Liberating Possibilities for Women* (2001)

This text uses a critical feminist lens to interpret women's experience of Ignatian Spirituality. It proposes new forms of prayer based on feminist interpretations of, for example, the thirty-day Silent Retreat created by Ignatius of Loyola.

24. McCoy—Ignatian Spirituality and Christian in *The Way*, 93, 91–106 (2015).

"Ignatian spirituality is about the direct encounter with God, which is always healing, and ultimately empowering. Feminism is about the full empowerment of the human person, which is healing. These two approaches are complementary and, when taken together, lead to greater healing and a richer experience of the Holy One" (92).

Appendix A

The Jesuit-Sponsored School Afterschool Program of Character Formation Student Survey

Grades 6–8 (2008–9)

Instructions for Taking This Survey

The following anonymous survey asks every Jesuit-Sponsored School student to answer a series of questions about the Jesuit-Sponsored School, the school day, the afterschool program, and in some cases, about life in general. The Jesuit-Sponsored School Afterschool Program of Character Formation is the program that you attend after the regular school day ends, which includes Encore, Study Hall, and Afternoon Assembly. (This survey is modeled after the *California Healthy Kids Survey 2005, California Department of Education After School Program Survey ASPS-Exit, Fall 2006, Grades 4–6.*)

- Your answers will help make the Jesuit-Sponsored School and the Jesuit-Sponsored School Afterschool Program of Character Formation better.
- There are no right or wrong answers. This is not a test.
- Please read every question carefully.
- Clearly mark all of your answers on the survey questionnaire.

Please do not write your name on this survey, this is an anonymous survey. We want your answers to stay private!

No one but you will know how you answered.

I. General Questions.

(Please circle your answer to the following questions.)

1. Please copy, in the space provided, today's date from the blackboard _____

2. Please copy, in the space provided, the time right now from the blackboard _____

3. How do you identify your race/ethnicity? (For other, please write-in the space provided, how you identify.)

    African American   Asian   Caucasian   Hispanic   Other:_____

4. How old are you?

    11 years old   12 years old   13 years old   14 years old

5. What grade are you in now?

    6th grade   7th Grade   8th Grade

6. Yesterday, how much time did you spend watching TV or playing video games?

    0) None, I didn't watch TV or play video games yesterday   1) Less than 1 hour
    2) About 1 hour   3) About 2 hours   4) 3 or more hours

7. When you are not in school, how often do you read books, magazines, or newspapers for fun?

    0) Almost never 1) A few times a week 2) A few times a month 3) Almost every day

8. Do you feel safe in the neighborhood where you live?
    (Safe means that you do not worry about random acts of violence happening to you.)
    0) No, never 1) Yes, some of the time 2) Yes, most of the time 3) Yes, all of the time

9. This school year, how many times have you hit or pushed other kids to hurt them during the Jesuit-Sponsored School's Afterschool Program of Character Formation when you were not just playing around?
    0) 0 times   1) 1 time   2) 2 times   3) 3 or more times

10. In how many classes did you receive less than the grade "C" during the 2nd Quarter?
    0) None   1) one   2) two   3) three   4) more than three

11. This school year, have you received a blue journal for behavioral probation?
    0) No   1) Yes

    If Yes, for how many quarters?
    1) 1   2) 2   3) 3

12. This school year, have you received a green journal for academic probation?
    0) No   1) Yes

    If Yes, for how many quarters?
    1) 1   2) 2   3) 3

II. Please respond freely and honestly to the following sets of questions about some of your experiences at the Jesuit-Sponsored School? (There are no right or wrong answers.)

13. Please describe how you make friends at the Jesuit-Sponsored School.

   _____
   _____
   _____
   _____

14. What makes you happy about attending the Jesuit-Sponsored School?

   _____
   _____
   _____
   _____

15. What are some of the ways that you participate in the Jesuit-sponsored school community (i.e., Service Saturdays and Lock-Ins)?

_____
_____
_____
_____

16. Please describe how you get along with members of the Jesuit-Sponsored School's other grades (i.e., 6th, 7th, 8th & Alumni)?

_____
_____
_____
_____

17. At the end of a school day, how do you feel about leaving the Jesuit-Sponsored School?

_____
_____
_____
_____

III. Questions about personal goals and abilities.

(Please circle your answer to the following questions.)

	No	Maybe	Yes
18. Can you do most things if you try?	0	1	2
19. Are there many things that you do well?	0	1	2
20. Do you have goals and plans for the future?	0	1	2
21. Do you plan to go to college or some other school after high school?	0	1	2
22. Have you ever thought about dropping out of school?	0	1	2

IV. How do you feel about the Jesuit-Sponsored School's Afterschool Program of Character Formation?

(Please circle your answer to the following questions.)

		None	Some	All
23.	Do you feel welcomed by teachers and staff to participate in all Encore activities?	0	1	2
24.	Does the Encore staff care about you?	0	1	2
25.	Does the Encore staff tell you when you do a good job?	0	1	2
26.	Does the Encore staff listen when you have something to say?	0	1	2
27.	Does the Encore staff believe that you can do a good job?	0	1	2
28.	Do you enjoy the other students in your Encore class?	0	1	2
29.	Are you happy to be at this Afterschool Program of Character Formation?	0	1	2
30.	Do you feel like you are a part of this Afterschool Program of Character Formation?	0	1	2
31.	Do you feel safe during the Afterschool Program of Character Formation?	0	1	2
32.	Do you help make rules or choose things to do?	0	1	2
33.	Do you do things to be helpful?	0	1	2

V. Questions about the activities in the Jesuit-Sponsored School's Encore Program.

(Please circle your answer to the following questions.)

		Never	Some of the time	Most of the time	All of the time
34.	Do you do things that you don't usually get to do?	0	1	2	3
35.	Do you do things that really make you think?	0	1	2	3
36.	Do the activities really interest you?	0	1	2	3

VI. On a scale of 1 to 10, with 1 equaling the least amount of time and 10 equaling the most amount of time:

During a normal week in the Jesuit-Sponsored School's Afterschool Program of Character Formation, how often do you do the following things?

(Please circle your answer to the following questions.)

37.	Homework	(Least) 1 2 3 4 5 6 7 8 9 10 (Most)
38.	Reading activities	(Least) 1 2 3 4 5 6 7 8 9 10 (Most)
39.	Writing activities	(Least) 1 2 3 4 5 6 7 8 9 10 (Most)
40.	Math/Science activities	(Least) 1 2 3 4 5 6 7 8 9 10 (Most)
41.	Arts activities (music, dance, art)	(Least) 1 2 3 4 5 6 7 8 9 10 (Most)
42.	Sports and games	(Least) 1 2 3 4 5 6 7 8 9 10 (Most)
43.	Pray/Talk to God	(Least) 1 2 3 4 5 6 7 8 9 10 (Most)

VII. How much has the Jesuit-Sponsored School's Afterschool Program of Character Formation helped you with any of these things?

(Please circle your answer to the following questions.)

		None	Very Little	Somewhat	Very Much
44.	Feel more like a part of your school	0	1	2	3
45.	Read better	0	1	2	3
46.	Write better	0	1	2	3
47.	Solve math or science problems	0	1	2	3
48.	Do better with your homework	0	1	2	3
49.	Make new friends	0	1	2	3
50.	Do better on your report card	0	1	2	3
51.	Get into less trouble at school	0	1	2	3
52.	Avoid fights	0	1	2	3
53.	Get along with others	0	1	2	3

54. Not use alcohol or other drugs	0	1	2	3
55. Learn to eat more nutritious food	0	1	2	3
56. Feel safer after school	0	1	2	3
57. Attend school more often	0	1	2	3

VIII. The Jesuit-Sponsored School student feedback.
(There are no right or wrong answers.)

58. Please name as many or as few activities that you would like added to the Jesuit-Sponsored School Encore Program.

   _____
   _____
   _____

59. Please provide any additional comments about things you like and dislike about the Jesuit-Sponsored School Afterschool Program of Character Formation (list as many or as few as you would like).

   _____
   _____
   _____

THANK YOU FOR TAKING THIS SURVEY!

Appendix B

Hypotheses

In response to my research questions the following hypotheses were generated:

The Afterschool Program of Character Formation (Encore Program) needs a more formal structure, one evidenced by a distinct and clear curriculum, the writing of goals and objectives to better ensure that it is meeting the Jesuit-Sponsored School's mission and purpose and to align the mission and purpose during future program evaluations.

The Jesuit-Sponsored School students are satisfied with the program, but can offer input, from their perspective on how to improve programming and to enhance the program's implementation and design.

Loyola students develop self-worth and self-esteem and discover new things about their selves through the Encore Program.

Encore Programming is flexible and meets student demand for activities.

The Encore Program intentionally creates an atmosphere conducive to youth development, including shared goals and long-term growth in student maturity.

Encore Program mentors and staff encourages their students to develop skills and emotional well-being.

The Encore Program is teaching students to love to learn and to integrate their identities as boys, as students from high-risk neighborhoods and communities.

All faculty/staff/administrators/parents are on board with the Encore Program and Encore Programming pedagogy.

Crime and violence in communities are reduced for student populations that remain actively involved and committed to afterschool programming (cf. the Youth Promise Act, 2009, H.R. 1064 at http://bobbyscott.house.gov/pdf/Crime_Summit_Packet_081203.pdf).

Appendix C

Results: Student Age and Self-Esteem

I. **Student Age and Self-Esteem (Chi-square)**
    Question: Does the Afterschool Program of Character Formation promote self-esteem?

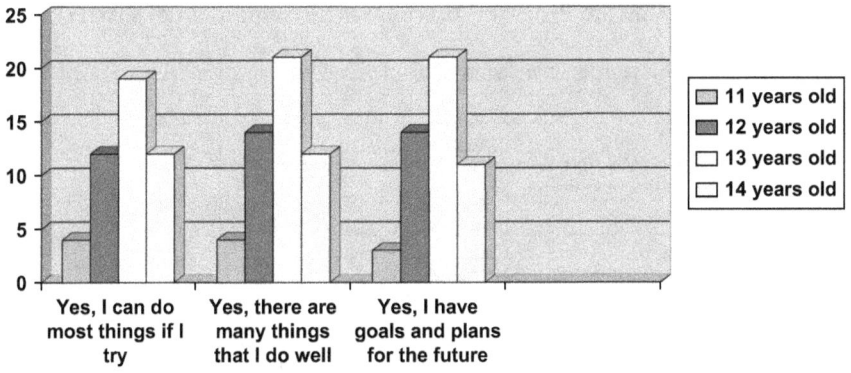

Appendix D

Results: Student Grade Level and Development of Social Skills

II. Student Grade Level (6, 7, and 8) and the Development of Social Skills (ANOVA)

Question: Does the Encore Program Afterschool Program of Character Formation (Encore Program) promote the development of social skills?

How much has the Jesuit-Sponsored School's Encore Program helped you . . .

		Mean Square	F	Sig.
Get into less trouble at school?				
	Between Groups	4.050	3.430	.040
	Within Groups	1.181		
Avoid Fights?				
	Between Groups	2.081	1.479	.238
	Within Groups	1.407		
Get along with others?				
	Between Groups	1.068	.898	.414
	Within Groups	1.190		
Make new friends?				
	Between Groups	5.689	6.793	.002
	Within Groups	.838		
Do better on your report card?				
	Between Groups	1.635	1.247	.296
	Within Groups	1.311		

The df for all questions is:
2
51
53

Comment: While the data suggested some significance in two of these questions, it would have been better to administer these questions in the recommended pretest/posttest format. In the student's mind, the Afterschool Program of Character Formation promotes less trouble at school but does not help them do better on their report card.

Appendix E

Results: Student Age and Intensity of Activity

III. **Student Age and Intensity of Activities Performed During the Afterschool Program of Character Formation (Encore Program) (Chi-Square)**

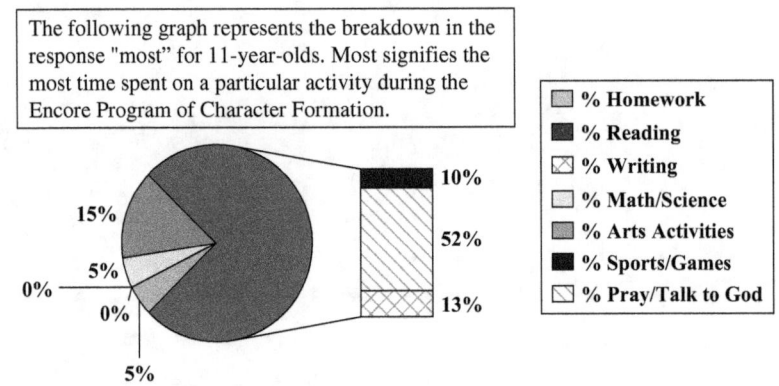

The following graph represents the breakdown in the response "most" for 11-year-olds. Most signifies the most time spent on a particular activity during the Encore Program of Character Formation.

- % Homework
- % Reading
- % Writing
- % Math/Science
- % Arts Activities
- % Sports/Games
- % Pray/Talk to God

10%
15%
52%
5%
0%
0%
13%
5%

Comment: Do the twelve-year-old responses evidence the Hawthorne Affect? 52 percent of twelve-year-olds spend most of their time during the Encore Program praying/talking to God; perhaps this indicates more exposure to religion and spirituality.

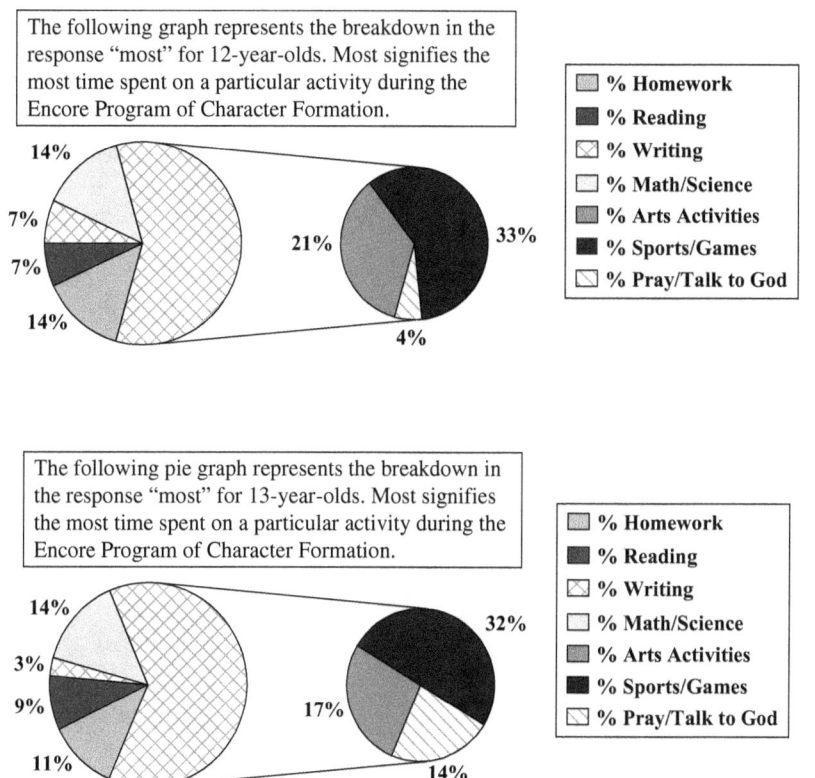

Appendix E

Comment: As age increases there seems to be greater similarities in how the students, age 12, 13, and 14 respond to what activities they spend the most time on. This could suggest greater connectivity among these peers' age groups.

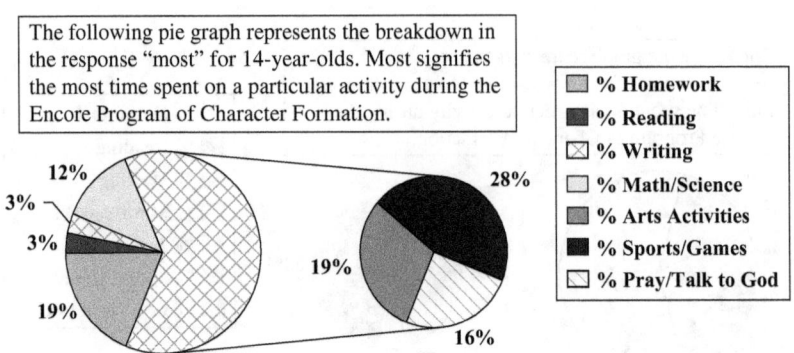

Appendix F

Results: Sense of Belonging

IV. Sense of Belonging among twelve and thirteen-year-olds in the Afterschool Program of Character Formation (Encore Program) (T-Test)

Question: Does the Encore Program increase students' age twelve and thirteen-years old sense of belonging?

Question	Age	N	Mean	T	Sig.	Mn Diff.
Do you feel welcomed by teachers and staff to participate in all Encore activities?	12	14	1.57	.149	.762	.026
	13	22	1.55	.148		
Does the Encore staff care about you?	12	14	1.64	.032	893	.006
	13	22	1.64	.031		
Does the Encore staff tell you when you do a good job?	12	14	1.71	1.171	.331	.169
	13	22	1.45	1.196		
Does the Encore staff listen when you have something to say?	12	14	1.21	.655	.331	.169
	13	22	1.05	.640		
Does the Encore staff believe that you can do a good job?	12	14	1.79	.933	.053	.149
	13	22	1.64	.965		
Do you enjoy the other students in your Encore class?	12	14	1.29	.736	.134	.123
	13	22	1.41	.748		
Are you happy to be at this Encore Program of Character Formation?	12	14	1.64	1.126	.112	.234
	13	22	1.41	1.202		

Appendix G
Logic Model Situation

The Jesuit-Sponsored School Afterschool Program of Character Formation is an afterschool program designed to help current students to succeed in life and in school, and to prepare them for further study in high school and college.

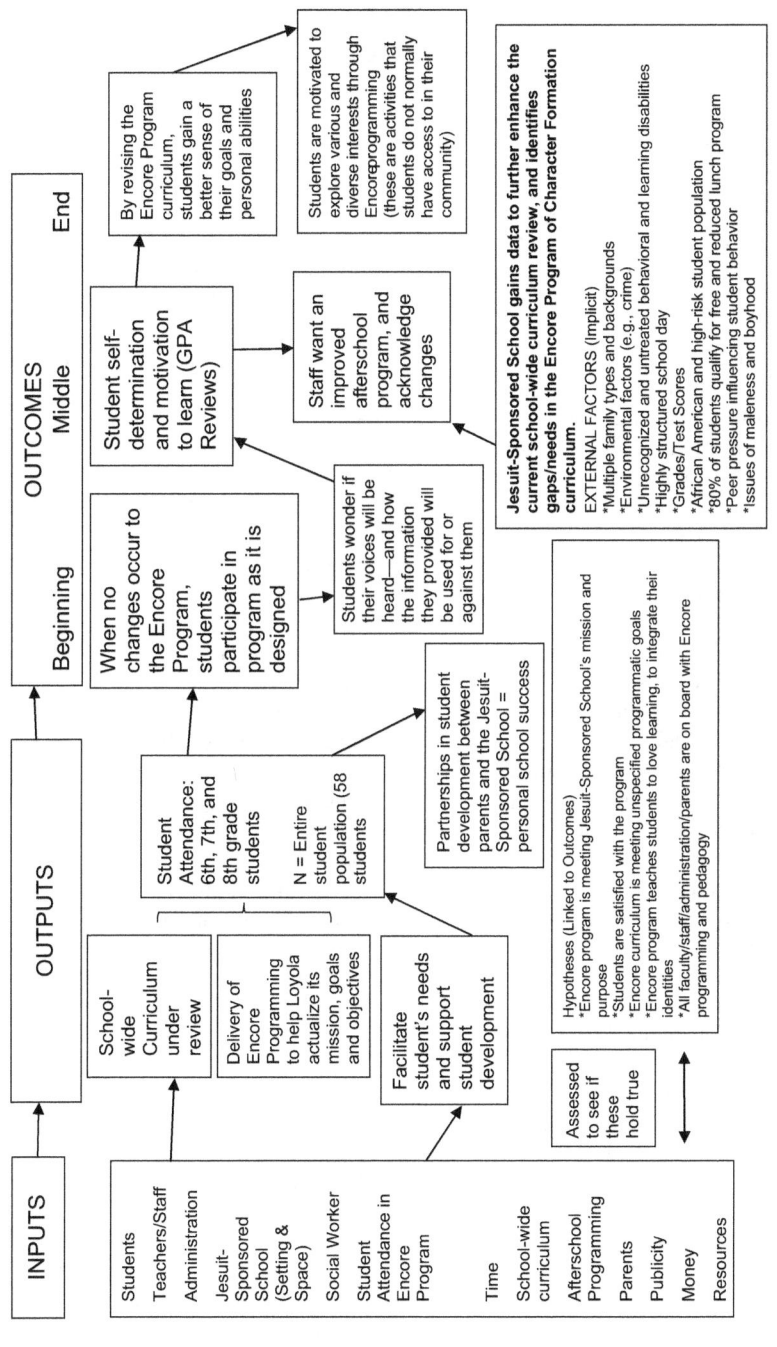

Index

accountability system 21, 23, 24
Acquaviva, Claudio 8
Ad maiorem Dei gloriam 4
Administration for Children and Families Child Care Bureau 52
African Americans 27, 50, 60, 90, 96, 99–102
afterschool education and programming 47, 49, 54, 63
   creating and sustaining 53
   curricula/curriculum 50, 52, 56
   design 51
   impacts of 51–2
   Missouri State Afterschool Profile and core content areas 52–3
Afterschool Education: Approaches to an Emerging Field (Noam, Biancarosa, and Dechausay) 50
Afterschool Investments Project (2009) 52
Afterschool Program of Character Formation 45, 63, 80
   afterschool education 50–4
   characteristics 49
   implications 60–1
   limitations 59–60
   methodology and research design 54–6
   objectives and background literature 48–9
   overview 47
   recommendations 62
   sense of belonging for twelve and thirteen years old 59
   student age and intensity of activities 58–9
   student age and self-esteem 56–7
   student grade level and development of social skills 57–8
Agape Love 14, 23, 42, 44, 109–11
Alexander, Karl L. 54

Amani, Cathy 21
Americans with Disabilities Act (ADA, 1990) 74
Angelou, Maya 98
Aquinas, St. Thomas 30
Aristotle 8, 125 n.7
Arrupe, Pedro 2
Association of Jesuit Colleges and Universities (AJCU) 4, 9
atheism 79
Augustine of Hippo 7

Baldwin, James 20, 96
Banks, David C. 4
behaviorism 2
Beloved Community 5, 6, 13, 23, 41, 85, 88, 91, 96, 97, 104, 105, 110, 111, 120 n.38
Berger, Ron 6
Biden, Joseph R. 7
Black Lives Matter Movement 1, 81
Blow, Charles M. 50
Blueprint for Improved Results for Students With Disabilities 70, 74
Blunt, Matt 53
Boryczka, Jocelyn 12
Boston School Age Child Care Project 53
Boyle, Gregory 14
"The Boys Are All Right" (von Drehle) 50
Boy Scouts of America 94
Boy Scouts of America v. Dale (2000) 94
Brackley, Dean 13, 75
Bushnell, Horace 29
Butler, Judith 12

California Department of Education After School Program Survey ASPS-Exit (2006) 47, 55
California Healthy Kids Survey (2005) 47, 55

Canada   9
Carson v. Makin (2022)   84
Catholic Counter Reformation   8
Catholic renewal   5
"*a certain Ignacianidad*"   2
Chapters on Moral Development
    (Kohlberg)   20
character, definition   20
"A Character" (Wordsworth)   6, 85
character formation   1–7, 3, 10, 11,
    12, 14, 17, 19–25, 28, 30–2,
    39, 40, 42, 44, 45, 47, 50, 52,
    54, 70, 77, 80–5, 91, 97,
    124 n.5
charter schools   4, 13, 42, 81, 82, 84
Child Care and Development Funds
    (CCDF)   52
chi-square   56–9
Christianitas   8
civil rights activists   102
Climate Change Movement   1
Common Core Standards/New York
    Next Generation Learning
    Standards   66
comparative theology   43
Comprehensive Education Plan   76
Cone, James   29, 97, 104, 108, 109
Congress to Unite Women the
    Radicalesbians   119 n.19
conscientization   28, 35, 44
Consolidated Plan   76
constructivism   2
contextual education   9, 22, 24, 42
Covid-19 pandemic   1, 5, 28, 44, 81, 89
Creating an Inclusive School (Villa and
    Thousand)   71
critical pedagogic theories   2
Cross and the Lynching Tree, The
    (Cone)   108
Cuban, Larry   14
cultural imperialism   89, 91
cultural revolution   35
cultural self-appropriation   84
cura apostolica   10, 23, 74
cura personalis   10, 19, 23, 24, 73–5, 80

Dalai Lama   108
Daly, Mary   29, 30, 32–8, 41, 44, 45,
    117 n.9

Dauber, Susan L.   54
de Bonifacio, Juan   3
de Jouvancy, Joseph   3
Descartes, René   8
Deutsch, Nancy L.   52, 53
Devereux Student Strengths Assessment
    (DESSA)   67
Dewey, John   9–11, 14, 20
Director of Formation   83
discrimination   38, 41, 43, 44, 87, 89, 90,
    95, 100, 105, 108, 109, 111
disunity   108
Dobbs v. Jackson Women's Health
    (2022)   28
Durkheim, Emile   116 n.19

Eastman, Crystal   36
education
    contextual   9
    democratization of   10
    formal   19, 20, 84
    general   3
    liberal classical   8
    philosophy   1, 8–10, 12, 14–16, 74
    private   3, 13, 17
    process   6
Edwards, Jonathan   29
Ellis, Havelock   33
ELL Periodic Assessments   70
Emancipatory Feminist Framework for
    Human Flourishing   36
emancipatory feminist theory of human
    flourishing   27, 30, 32, 37, 43,
    44, 80, 117–18 n.9, 119 n.19
Emdin, Christopher   29
Encore Afterschool Education and
    Enrichment Program   63
Encore Character Formation
    Program   27, 54, 58–9, 62
English Language Learners (ELLs)   4, 66
Entwisle, Doris R.   54
epistemology   36, 96
    critical social inquiry   99–100
    forms of knowledge   97–8
    knowledge of socially constructed
        categories and social
        world   98–9
Equal Rights Amendment   35
Erasmus of Rotterdam   8

Espinosa v. Montana Board of Revenue (2020)   29
Establishment Clause of First Amendment   6
Ethical Demands of Integration, The (King)   94
Ethic of Care   31
ethics
  avoiding treating people as mere means/children   102
  bad and good shame   104–5
  disagreement calls for dialogue   102–4
  overview   100–1
ethnic stratification systems   89
evangelization   25
Eve   40
Eve-il   40, 41
Everson v. Board of Education (1947)   29
evil   33, 39–41, 43, 88, 106–7
Experiment in Love, An (King)   109
extremism   10, 23, 43, 104, 108, 109

factionalism   43, 87, 104, 108, 109
faith and pedagogy   27–31, 43–5, 81
Family Educational Rights and Privacy Act (FERPA, 1974)   74
Fashola, Olatokunbo S.   52, 53
federal law   71
Federal/State Free and Reduced Lunch Program   60
feminism   28, 30, 31, 35, 38
  radical   35, 36
  regressive   35
  wave of   31, 35
feminist flourishing   118 n.9
feminist inquiry   38
feminist theologians   25, 29, 30, 45, 81
feminist theology and pedagogy   5, 27–45
feminist theory   31
Fiore, Nina   53, 54
Fire Next Time, The (Baldwin)   20
Fletcher, Hill   118 n.9
forgiveness   41, 106–7
Formula of the Institute   7
Francis I (Pope)   7, 108
Free Speech and Free Exercise Clause of First Amendment   6

Freire, Paulo   23, 28, 44
fundamentalism   104, 108
Funds of Knowledge: Theorizing Practice in Household (González, Moll and Amani)   21, 79

Galtung, Johan   95
Gamberini, Paolo   82
Gandhi, Mohandas K.   88–91, 98, 100, 105, 108–11
Gardner, Howard   20
Gay and Lesbian Liberation Movement   31
globalism   1
global War on Terrorism   41, 42, 108
God   25
  belief/faith in   40
  contemplation of   120 n.35
  existence   106
  as feminine/mother   25, 38–9
  relationship with human being   8, 12, 15–16
  as Truth   105
  will of   88, 90, 111
González, Norma   21, 79
group identity   93, 94
guilt   94–6
Gyn/Ecology (Daly)   34

Hall, Radclyffe   29, 30, 32–5, 39, 41, 44, 45, 117 n.9, 118 n.14
Hawthorne effect   59
Healthy Lifestyles programming   53
hermeneutics   24, 28, 30, 31, 33, 35, 38, 81
Heschel, Abraham Joshua   88
Hill Fletcher, Jeannine   29, 30, 32, 33, 36, 39–45, 117 n.9
homosexuals   94, 96, 99
Hugo, Victor   31
Hull, Ernest R.   20
human development   14, 23, 110
human flourishing   6, 10, 12–14, 19, 23, 27, 30–3, 37, 39, 41–3, 45, 47, 52, 56, 70, 71, 80, 82, 83, 87–92, 97, 100–10, 116 n.19, 117–18 n.9, 118 n.14, 119 n.19, 124 n.5, 128 n.35
human good   33, 91

humanism 16
Humanist Tradition 1, 8, 16, 84
humanity 13, 17, 23, 42, 90, 94, 108, 110
human life 89
human nature 91
   endowments 91–2
   family 93
   group membership 93–4
   structural violence 94–6
human relationships 22–4, 34, 80

I Am Not Your Negro (Baldwin) 20
I Care A Lot (2021) 31
Ignatian Pedagogical Paradigm (*IPP*) 3, 5, 9, 10, 12–14, 17, 20, 24, 27, 30, 32, 34, 38, 41–5, 47, 50, 54, 55, 60, 62, 63, 65–7, 71–7, 80–4, 91, 105, 111
Ignatian Pedagogy 2, 3, 5, 7, 10, 11, 13–14, 17, 23, 24, 31, 47, 66, 67, 71–7, 79–84, 91, 105, 111
Ignatian Spirituality 7, 10, 14, 17, 25, 36, 80–3, 124 n.5
Ignatius of Loyola 1, 2, 4, 5, 39, 81, 82, 105, 111, 125 n.12
   and character formation 19–25
   educational ideals 11–13
   experience of God 7, 15, 80
   Ignatian Pedagogical Paradigm (*IPP*) 13–14
   pedagogy of 7–11, 22, 25, 32, 42, 54, 80, 81, 83–5
   spiritual concepts influencing educational philosophy 14–16
Individualized Education Plan (IEP) 65, 67, 70, 73, 75
Individuals with Disabilities Act (IDEA, 1975) 74
Industrial Revolution 1, 28
Integrated Co-Teaching (ICT) 68, 70–2, 76
intellectual activity 91, 92
intergalactic journey 32, 33, 36
internal religious diversity 43
International Baccalaureate Program 3
International Commission on Apostolate of Jesuit Education 71
interpersonal relationships 98
interreligious dialogue 30, 33, 36, 40–3, 108–10, 120 n.39

interreligious encounters 42
interreligious interconnectivity 14, 23, 33, 40, 42, 43, 108–10, 120 n.39
interreligious solidarity 40
intersectionality 90
i-Ready 70

James, William 29
Jefferson, Thomas 29
Jesuit and Feminist Education (Boryczka and Petrino) 12
Jesuit Colleges 9
Jesuit Cristo Rey Schools 9
Jesuit education 2, 3, 7–9, 13, 41, 47, 54, 67, 73, 77, 80, 84
Jesuit High Schools 9
Jesuit Nativity Miguel Partner School 63
Jesuit Nativity Schools 9
Jesuit Order 16
Jesuit school program/model 2, 3
Jesuit Schools Network (JSN) 2, 9
Jesuit Secondary Education Association (JSEA). *See* Jesuit Schools Network (JSN)
Jesuit-Sponsored Schools 2, 4, 5, 7, 9, 20, 24, 25, 27, 28, 40, 44, 45, 47–50, 53–6, 59–63, 73, 80, 90
Jesuit-Sponsored School Student Survey 55
Jim Crow laws 100
Johnson, Elizabeth 29, 30, 32, 33, 36, 38, 39, 41, 44, 45, 117 n.9
Joseph A. Kennedy v. Bremerton School District (2022) 6

Kansas and Missouri Core Competencies for Youth Development Professionals 52
Kant, Immanuel 13
King, Martin Luther, Jr. 13, 88, 91, 93–8, 104–8, 110, 111, 116 n.19
knowledge 96, 97
   experiential 37
   knowing-how, knowing-that, knowing-you 97–8
   propositional 37, 97–8
   relational 98
   scientific 98

of socially constructed categories 98–9
Kohlberg, Lawrence 20
Kolbe, Kathy 75
Kolvenbach, Peter-Hans 67
Kugel, James 29
Ku Klux Klan 94, 101, 106
Kulis, Stephen 89
Kumpfer, Karol L. 51

labels/labeling 37, 38, 42, 94, 96, 99–101. *See also* negative labeling
Lauver, Sherri 51
Lavender Menace 119 n.19
Lazear, David 20
Least Restrictive Environment (LRE) 5, 27, 63, 65–7, 72–6, 81
Lee, Harper 99
lesbianism 33
lesbians 32, 34, 35, 119 n.19
Les Miserables (Hugo) 31
Levene Test for Equality of Variances 59
LGBTQ+ people 90
liberation 41, 44
liberationism 2
Locke, John 12
Los Angeles' Better Educated Students for Tomorrow 53
Louisiana 27
"Love, Law, and Civil Disobedience" (King) 95
Lowell, James Russell 106
L Word, The (2004, TV series) 31

MacKinnon, Catharine 12
MAGA Movement 100
Magis 4, 10–11, 71, 82, 111
male-centered critical theory 28
Mann, Horace 14
marginalization 33, 44, 89–91, 95
Marsiglia, Flavio 89
Maryland 27
Masters of Sex (2013, TV series) 31
Math, Engineering, Technology, and Science (METS) programming 53
Maynard, Rebecca A. 51
Measure of Student Learning (MoSL) 70
Merton, Robert 126 n.4, 127 n.15

metaethics 32, 35, 36
meta-patriarchy 36
#MeToo Movement 1, 81
Metts, Ralph E. 20, 54
"middle of the road" approach 71, 72
Miller, B. M. 54
Missouri 52
Missouri Afterschool Action Plan 52
Missouri Afterschool Program Self-Assessment tool 52
Missouri Afterschool Program Standards 52
Missouri Afterschool Resource Center 52
Missouri Province of the Society of Jesus 54
Missouri State Afterschool Profile 51–3
Missouri Statewide Afterschool Network 53
Moliere 8
Moll, Luis C. 21
moral evil 128–9 n.43
moral suffering 106
"The Most Durable Power" (King) 110
Most Restrictive Environment (MRE) 5, 27, 63, 65, 72, 73, 81
motherhood as metaphor 32, 33, 36, 42
Motherhood as Metaphor (Hill Fletcher) 39
multicultural education 24, 42
multilingual learners 66
Multi-Tiered System of Supports (MTSS) 76
mutual recognition 14, 23, 41–3, 90, 91, 101, 103, 104, 107–10, 120 n.42

Nativity Network 48
Nativity School 48
negative labeling 37, 42, 43, 87, 99–101, 108, 109
negative stereotypes 37, 108, 120 n.37
neutral education system 44
New York City 1, 4
New York City Beacons 53
New York City Department of Education (NYC DOE) 2–7, 12, 13, 30, 31, 39, 40, 42, 65, 67, 72, 80, 87, 124 n.5

New York City Public School   3, 5–7, 19, 21, 25, 27, 38, 43, 45, 77, 80, 81
   academic success and student flourishing   70–3
   adopting/adapting Ignatian Pedagogy   11
   challenges and growth   73–4
   demographics and place of practice   66–7
   evidence of impact   75–6
   expanding discourse   81–2
   Ignatian Pedagogy and *IPP*   74–5
   implications and findings   79–81
   overview   65–6
   presupposition   68–70
   recommended special education program   70, 76
   students   4, 9, 10, 14, 76, 80, 82
   teachers at   75–6
New York's East Side Boys and Girls Clubs   53
New York State Education Department   70
New York State English Language Arts (NYS ELA)   70
New York State Math (NYS Math)   70
New York Times   50
Nicomachean Ethics (Aristotle)   125 n.7
Noam, Gil   52–4
No Child Left Behind Act (NCLB, 2002)   74
"No More Excuses?" (Blow)   50
noncooperation   94
nontraditional family   93, 105
nonviolent weapon   94
North American Jesuit-Sponsored Schools   2
Notes of a Native Son (Baldwin)   96
nuclear family   34, 93
NYC DOE School Quality Guide (2018-19)   65, 66
NYSAA   70

objectification   102
One-Way ANOVA   56–8
ontic suffering   106
oppression/oppressive practices   1, 29, 39, 88–91
Orange Is the New Black (2013, web series)   31
Other   10, 25, 40

Parent Association (PA)   66
parent coordinator (PC)   66
paternalism   102
Paul, Alice   36
Pavur, Claude   84
pedagogy, definition   27
personal identity   101
Peters, Richard Stanley   7
Petrino, Elizabeth   12
Philip II (King of Spain)   8
philosophical theology   35, 38
philosophy of God
   overview   105–6
   reducing effects of evil   106–7
philosophy of religion
   interreligious dialogue and interreligious interconnectivity   108–10
   overview   105–6
Pius VII (Pope)   8
Polanco, Juan   16
postmodernism   31
Pre-Kindergarten Turning-5 (T5) process   72, 73
private schools   6, 13, 44, 82, 84
proto-feminism   30
public school education   1–7, 3, 10, 12, 21, 25, 29, 30, 32, 42. *See also* New York City Public School
   faith and   30, 43–5, 81
   free   27, 29, 84
   God-speak in   28, 38, 39, 42, 79
   process   29
   students   7, 9, 10, 14, 40, 44
   system   28, 44, 80–2, 84
   urban   13, 79, 81

race   88–9
racism   89
Radicalesbians   35
"Radical Feminism: The Qualitative Leap Beyond Patriarchal Religion" (Daly)   36
Ratio Studiorum (*RS*)   5, 8–10, 12, 14, 16, 84

Regimini Militantis Ecclesiae 7
Regina v. Wilde (1895) 34
religious freedom 6
religious identities 43
Renaissance 8, 28
respect 14, 23, 41–3, 67, 90, 91, 101–5, 107–10, 120 n.42
Response to Intervention (RTI) 76
Ribadneira, Pedro 8
Rich, Adrienne 36
Roe v. Wade (1973) 28, 103
Roman Catholic Bishops 28
Roman Catholic Church 1, 27, 90
Roman Catholic Magisterium 30, 33
Roman Catholic Schools 12, 27, 28
Rousseau, Jean Jacques 13
RULER 67
Rules for Thinking with the Church (Ignatius of Loyola) 2
Running Records 70

St. Frances Academy 27
Saint Peter's Preparatory School 2, 21
same-sex sexual desire 33, 35
Sanford Harmony 67
Satyagraha. See nonviolent weapon
Scholastic Tradition 8
School-Based Support Team 73
Second International Symposium on Belief (1975) 36
secularism 79
self-determination 54, 61–3, 92, 105
self-esteem 5, 47, 53, 56–7, 61, 67, 90, 91, 103
self-fulfilling prophecy 126 n.4
self-rule 92, 105, 111
self-worth 47, 53, 67, 90, 91, 94
Seligman, Martin E. P. 51
Sen, Amartya 116 n.19
Seneca Falls Convention 31
sense of belonging 56, 59, 60, 62, 63, 67, 109
Sex and the City (1998, TV series) 31
sexual disability 33
sexual identity 33
Shakur, Tupac 101
shame 44, 94–6, 104–5, 108, 111
She Who Is (Johnson) 38
slavery 1, 39, 92

social activism 88
social constructivism 2
social-emotional intelligence 5, 22, 61, 67
social injustice 88
socialization 35, 51, 93, 99, 127 n.15
social justice 9, 31
social skills 57–8, 61, 77
Society of Jesus 1, 2, 7, 8, 11, 20, 90
Sollicitudo Omnium Ecclesiam 8
Southern White racists 102, 107
Spanish Missions 27
special education law 71
Spiritual Exercises (Ignatius of Loyola) 2, 3, 7, 10, 80, 83, 105
Stanton, Elizabeth Cady 118 n.9
Strictly 4 My N.I.G.G.A.Z. (1993, album) 101
Stride Towards Freedom (King) 96
structural violence 37, 41, 43, 44, 88–90, 94–6, 105, 108–11, 127–8 n.22
Student and Family Handbook 48, 62
student(s)
  academic achievement 69, 70, 76, 82
  at-risk 50
  First Amendment rights 29
  learning 2–3, 6, 9, 21, 22, 24, 29, 53, 54, 60, 61, 67, 71, 76, 81
  parents involved in curriculum 73–5
  participation in afterschool programming 51, 52
  prayer life 61
students with disabilities (SWDs) 4, 27, 65–7, 71, 74, 75
Swaraj. See self-rule
systemic harm 95, 110
systemic violence 13, 20

Taylor, Charles 19
Teachers College, Columbia University 21, 29, 101
Teachers College Reading and Writing Project (TCRWP) 66, 70
Thatamanil, John J. 110
Thousand, Jacqueline 71
Time Magazine 50
Tinkering Toward Utopia (Tyack and Cuban) 14
To Kill a Mockingbird (Lee) 99

traditional family   34, 93
tribalism   43, 104, 108, 109
Trigger Laws   103
Trump, Donald J.   100
t-test   59
Tyack, David   14

United States   9, 27, 31, 52, 87
United States of America Federal Law   74
US Civil Rights Movement   31, 102, 104
US Constitution   6, 29, 44
US Department of Health and Human Services   52
US Supreme Court   6, 12, 28, 29, 84, 94, 103

Valley Stream Central School District   1
Vicky Cristina Barcelona (2008)   31
Villa, Richard   71
virtue   116 n.19
Voltaire   8
von Drehle, David   50

Weissberg, Roger P.   51
Well of Loneliness, The (Hall)   32–5, 39
Where Do We Go From Here? (King)   107
Wilde, Oscar   34
Williams, Roger   29
Wittig, Monique   37
women
   equality/inequality   31, 118 n.9
   experience of God   45
   in male-dominated society   28, 31, 35, 36
   and pedagogy   30
   reproductive rights   28
   rights movements   118 n.9
   sexual liberation of   31
Wordsworth, William   6, 85

Yale Center for Emotional Intelligence   67
Yancy, George   50

Zief, Susan Goerlich   51, 54

www.ingramcontent.com/pod-product-compliance
Lightning Source LLC
Chambersburg PA
CBHW052124300426
44116CB00010B/1776